TABLE OF CONTENTS

To Joanie — My partner in every way

INTRODUCTION

"I had a great idea for a seminar. I spent a lot of time planning a good program and researching the market. I am extremely well qualified to teach, and I'm a good speaker, but I just couldn't get anyone to come to my sessions. Now I see where another operation is doing a seminar on the same subject, and they're taking it all over the country. It looks like a resounding success. What I want to know is, where did I go wrong?"

This refrain has become a familiar one to me after eighteen years in the seminar and workshop business. Worthwhile programs come and go, often with little apparent connection between the quality of a presentation and its success. In the over-200,000 participant training days I have planned, managed, and conducted, I am constantly struck by one important point: <u>Success in the seminar and workshop business is much more a function of marketing and promotion than it is the result of program design, materials development, and instructional competency.</u>

To be sure, long-term success requires a quality program, good materials, and effective instruction. There exists a substantial body of literature to help develop these for your own program. This book does not attempt to duplicate this information, although it does discuss, in some detail, a cost-effective approach to program development. Good materials and effective instruction alone are not sufficient for success. The landscape is littered with hapless inventors who have spent years developing and fine-tuning what they consider to be "the finest training program or seminar on the subject in the history of mankind." And they may be right. But if it does not sell, they wind up broke, discouraged and bitter.

This book concentrates on the successful marketing of seminars, workshops, and related educational events. It

5

discusses the marketing of open-to-the-public seminars and workshops -- in which pursuit about three-fourths of my training days have been spent -- and captive training programs undertaken (by consultants and trainers) for corporate and other organizational clients, or employers, which have occupied the balance of my training time. Attention here is given to:

a) the differences between various kinds of programs
b) marketing strategies that are appropriate for your program
c) test-marketing
d) establishing a price and break-even point
e) the use of contracts
f) ways to obtain seminar materials without developing them yourself.

It focuses on the practical problems that confront a seminar developer and promoter, and realistic, cost-effective solutions.

The potential for success in this business is enormous. The demand for continuing adult education and training is substantial and growing every day. One source estimates that the adult post-formal training market in the United States is a six-billion-dollar-a-year industry. Although it is certainly a competitive business, it is also a diverse one with room for competition. An industry fee range of between $20 and $500 per day indicates a flexible market that will accommodate innovation and a demand for programs that often goes unmet.

My purpose in writing this book is to help you create and market a successful seminar or workshop that will share in the rewards of this booming industry. It will teach you how to insure that the program in which you invest your money, time and energies will succeed. If you heed its lessons, which are based on my work and the experience of others in the field, it can keep you from swelling the ranks of the hapless inventors.

(To avoid awkward sentence structure, the male pronoun is used throughout the book; this should be understood to imply both sexes.)

Chapter 1
GETTING STARTED

There is no better testament to the strength of the American entrepreneurial spirit than the seminar and workshop business. Successful programs abound, on every topic from how to communicate with your boss to how to commune with your subconscious mind. If you want to learn about tax incentives while dining on lobster in a restaurant atop a revolving tower, someone, somewhere, has designed a program with you in mind. You can attend low-budget lectures in borrowed auditoriums or opulent weekend sessions in which the agenda seems to consist mostly of swimming, golfing and tennis opportunities. There are seminars so rigidly constructed that participants are told when to go to the bathroom, and workshops so open-ended that one would be hard-pressed to identify a leader or a plan.

Where, in this myriad of enterprises, does one begin to look for clues as to why some prosper and others fail? And what steps can you take to ensure the success of your own venture? There are no easy answers, in spite of the crystal-ball gazers who tell you otherwise. These so-called experts are applying a formula to a business that defies standardization by its very diversity. The lack of uniformity, however, does not mean that it is impossible to gauge, with some degree of accuracy, the likely public response to a program. You do not have to risk your life-savings in one dramatic gamble. The potential for profit can be measured and the risk of failure held to a minimum by careful planning; and the initial investment can be held to a modest, definable amount.

There are a couple of ways to take the pulsebeat of your embryonic venture before it emerges fully grown. **Conducting market research** is one way of exploring the viability of an idea before committing resources to its development. Market research is frequently conducted by designing and using a questionnaire to measure a potential participant's likely response to a given situation. To garner information useful in developing a program agenda, you would probably want to ask your respondents whether or not they would attend a seminar on the topic you've chosen, how much they would be willing to pay to attend, and what kinds of activities they think should be included. Market research is most useful in a contract or "captive" training program, one done under contract to an organizational client. When the information requested is specific and factual, such as in what areas potential attendees would like further training to do their jobs more effectively, market research can be an efficient method of garnering meaningful data.

Another way to gauge the potential for success is to **test-market** the program; that is, actually promote and conduct the seminar or workshop, and evaluate the results. Although this method may seem to be costlier and riskier than conducting market research, it is most often less expensive because it provides a much firmer foundation upon which to build long-range plans when a program (non-captive) appeals to the general public or business community.

Market research measures expectations of behavior; test-marketing measures the behavior itself. There is normally a world of difference between what people say they would do and their actual behavior in a given situation. Most people like to think of themselves as the kind of individuals who would attend a seminar to enhance their personal or professional growth. They want others to think this of them as well. So, if you are presentable and polite when you ask your questions, they can flatter their self-image and make you happy at the same time by telling you exactly what you want to hear. If you believe the results of this kind of "market research" you will soon be convinced that you are living in the best of all possible worlds and that your program can't fail. Unless the information you seek is so straightforward that there is likely to be little discrepancy between plan and action, market research can result in some mistaken beliefs. The results of test-marketing, on the other hand, reflect decisions influenced by such pragmatic factors as tight budgets, crowded schedules, previous commitments; in short, all the elements that enter into real-world decisions.

What exactly does test-marketing accomplish? It provides a basis upon which to make sound judgments about the likely public response to a program, i.e. its chances of success. Conducting a program under test conditions (which are discussed in detail in chapter six), permits field-testing in a location that has the advantages of high media efficiency and low cost, but that otherwise replicates the conditions found in places that will eventually host your seminar. Therefore, predictions can be made with reasonable accuracy about the behavior of future markets, based upon the responses of a test-market. Changes made on the basis of test-marketing evaluations should "travel" well and receive a consistent reaction from audiences everywhere. The ability of a program to adapt to changing locations and circumstances is called the **roll-out.** For instance, if you are going to conduct a workshop on the rent-control laws of Los Angeles, you may get an excellent turnout in Los Angeles. But you will not be able to take that workshop to Denver, Chicago, or New York without researching those cities' rent-control laws, i.e. developing a whole new concept. When planning an agenda and assembling materials, make sure that they are not limited to the interests of a specific group, location or time-frame. The same program should be usable, with only minor modifications, on every occasion that it is presented.

With low overhead and start-up costs, seminar developers and promoters can test-market programs very inexpensively. A test-run of a session that is open to the general public or business community can cost as little as $600. A captive program can be tested for even less. The seminar/workshop business is characterized by low cost, low risk investment with a high asset value, and the two keys to unlocking this fortuitous combination of events are:
I. Getting the best value for your promotional dollars.
2. Testing before investing.

Getting the best value. Approximately two-thirds of the total cost of presenting a seminar is spent on the deceptively simple enterprise of generating interest and attrracting particiants to a program. The effectiveness of a marketing campaign -- the depth and breadth of the coverage your promotional budget buys -- is the largest single factor in the future success or failure of a program. If you are advertising in a newspaper, you must ascertain that the ad will actually be read by a segment of

9

the populace that is going to be most interested in your seminar. If you are using direct mail, you must target your most likely participants before sending out expensive brochures. There are techniques that will increase the effectiveness of your promotion and shave dollars off its cost at every turn (these are explored in chapters two and three). Only through an understanding of the media and a conscientious effort to measure actual media performance, dollar for dollar, against its expected return, can you determine the best promotional values. Staying alert to the pulling power of your marketing efforts will enable you to cut your losses quickly on advertising channels that do not result in a sufficient number of registrants to justify their cost. The results of test-marketing provide a realistic standard by which to measure the efficiency of your promotions rather than broad estimates based on other programs that may or may not be valid for your situation.

Testing before investing. This is a truth well understood by some book publishers, who sometimes advertise a book before it is even written to test the pulling power of a subject. If the response is good, the author and printer get the go-ahead to proceed, and the orders are fulfilled. If the idea doesn't sell well enough, the few who were enticed by the ad are told that the book will not be available, and the money is refunded. This technique in not entirely practical for your purposes, unless the prospect of telling a room full of registrants, "I'm sorry, there s really no seminar. I just wanted to see if you'd show up." doesn't cause you the slightest consternation. But the risk-minimizing principle applies: test the concept of a program before making substantial investments in development and materials. Your early sessions should be inexpensive and simply designed, for two reasons:
1. So that you can change various elements of the agenda quickly and inexpensively in response to changing cir-cumstances and early feedback.
2. To conserve capital so that the marketing approach can be changed and tested again, if the initial sessions do not result in the expected number of participants.
  Unlike General Motors, you shouldn't have to spend millions of dollars in order to chart basic changes in your future path. If your fledgling effort is not burdened with topheavy development costs, it will fly with only a modest investment. Travel light to retain the ability to make

changes inexpensively.

Keeping the agenda of a seminar straightforward during the test-marketing phase is sound planning for more than economic reasons. First, because the developer does not have a large financial or ego investment in the status quo, he is far more likely to be amenable to suggestions for innovations that will shape the future growth of the program. This kind of flexibility and willingness to make active changes based on responsible feedback is necessary if a program is to benefit from a continuing participant-developer dialogue. Second, an agenda that grows in this fashion has a better chance of being on target with the needs of its market than one that is developed in isolation from the dynamics of field-testing.

An open-minded attitude towards change should extend to all aspects of the program, not just the program agenda and marketing. Some of the variables that contribute to the overall success and quality of a session are:

1. The topic itself. Is there a large enough, readily identifiable population with a sustained interest in the topic you've chosen?

2. Geographic and regional variations. Will your seminar do better in some regions of the country than in others, and will it have the greatest appeal to people in rural areas, suburbanites, or city-dwellers within a given region?

3. Price sensitivitty. Will your fee be regarded as too high in some places, and not enough in others?

4. Location. To what degree will the location and facility in which you hold your sessions affect the way the public perceives the program?

5. Time of day. Should you schedule your session in the evenings so that people can attend after work, or during the day so that they must miss work to attend? Should you schedule on weekdays or weekends?

6. Length of program. A few hours, or a few days? How does this affect the way your program is received and the fee you can charge?

All these elemental variables, and others, can and should be tested by varying them from session to session, one at a time (so that you are not comparing apples and oranges in your analysis), and comparing the results. This fine-tuning process should continue throughout the life of a program if it is to stay vital, but it is important in the early stages, when your program's future survival could

11

well depend on a rapid response to changing conditions.

How to choose a topic. The selection of a topic for your seminar or workshop should be shaped by the needs of your prospective participants and your own interests. Find a subject that people are generally interested in, or one in which they need more information. If you will be presenting the information yourself, the topic you choose should be one that is dear to your heart and about which you are knowledgeable. If a subject is boring to you, presenting the information will quickly become dull, time-consuming drudgery. The best subject is one that you are so familiar with that you could talk intelligently about it for several days on a moment's notice. You will also be in a better position to develop more sophisticated materials and improve the presentation, because the topic is intrinsically interesting. After all, one of the primary benefits of developing your own program is that it frees you from the rules of others who are no longer in a position to dictate your choices in life. So why not pick a topic that you'll enjoy discussing for several hours on a daily or weekly basis?

Is there a long-term demand for information on the topic you're considering? Some topics have too limited an appeal to be viable. For example, a seminar on how to sell your own house wothout a broker would probably not succeed ---for two reasons: First, the total universe of people interested in selling their homes at any given time is very limited; once the house is sold, they no longer inhabit that participant universe; also, the public has no interest in such a seminar prior to their interest in selling, after they have sold, or after they have turned to a broker. Second, people who are trying to save a realtor's commission are unlikely candidates to spend money on seminars and workshops; such a topic might be more appropriate for a book. Choose a topic in which the potential participants have a long-term sustained interest.

What kind of information are people willing to pay for? If a workshop promises to help them become more successful or make more money, it will be viewed as cost-effective, and they will pay for it out of their own pockets. Individuals will not pay for training which appears to benefit someone else more than themselves. The party who benefits from the improved skills, often the employer, is expected to pay in these situations.

Another factor in selecting a topic is the availability
of other ways to obtain the same information. The subjects
of almost every seminar and workshop given in the United
States today are covered by a myriad of other, usually less
expensive, sources: books, jounals, magazines, videotapes,
audio cassettes, and other types of media. Seminars and
workshops continue to thrive in spite of this because they
are an easy and efficient way to learn. It is,
nevertheless, wise to be aware of other sources available
on your topic, since these publications and materials are
competing with your presentation as a source of
information.

Is there competition for your idea? If there are no
other programs available anywhere on the subject, that may
be a signal that your topic is not suitable for a seminar,
rather than a signal that you have the entire lucrative
field to yourself. It is unlikely that someone else has not
thought of and tested your idea. Unlikely, but not
impossible, so don't dismiss the idea yet. There are a few
classic cases of overnight success where someone finds and
develops an untapped market, but there are far more
instances where a total lack of competition means that
there is not enough interest in the topic to support a
seminar. Some competition may be helpful. If others are
delivering successful seminars, there may be room in the
market for you. You may be able to obtain your own niche or
segment of the market which is not adequately served by
competitors. A great deal of competition is probably
unhealthy. It may suggest a market overrun with competition
or one which is about tapped out (too mature).

Who Pays? The choice of topic will largely determine
whether your program will be paid for by the participant
himself or some benefactor, such as an employer. A seminar
or workshop will likely be paid for by the participant
himself with his won funds if it has any of the following
characteristics:
1. It provides information which enables the participant
   to make more money. Seminars on how to buy foreclosure
   property, how to invest in the stock market, or how to
   start your own direct-mail marketing business are all
   eminently salable as public programs.
2. It appeals to avocational interests or recreational
   desires. Travel, sewing, cooking and scuba-diving are
   all examples of this. People are generally willing to

spend money on their leisure-time pursuits.
3. It offers techniques and strategies for personal growth self-awareness, and dealing effectively with others in multiple walks of life. It offers benefits which the participants feel will be helpful in both their personal and professional lives. Sensitivity training, communication effectiveness workshops, stress analysis sessions, leadership seminars, marriage-encounter groups, and assertiveness training programs are all pertinent examples.

A program will likely be paid for by a benefactor if it has any of these features:
1. The training or information is perceived to be of greater value to someone other than the participant. The participant's attitude is, "It is my boss, not I, who will benefit from this training, so let him pay for it." Programs on organizational communications or business writing, for instance, often fall into this category.
2. The improved skills offered benefit the individual personally or professionally, but do not have direct economic impact on the participant. Seminars on time management and planning are good examples of this.
3. The material is uninteresting to the potential participant. There is some information that people simply need to know, but that is so boring they're certainly not going to spend their own money to acquire it. For example, a program on how to design an information system is very useful, but quickens the pulse of few.

Success for a public seminar or workshop requires that the program be perceived by the potential participant (or benefactor) as an effective way of mastering a body of material. In a seminar situation, people can absorb a lot of pratical and highly-focused information in a short period of time. The seminar setting, audio-visual supports, and written material all serve to reinforce the learning process and make it a relatively painless way to learn. If, however, it appears to be more convenient and desirable to read a book or obtain the same information from another source, the public will do so.

A public seminar further requires that your likely participant will be comfortable in a seminar setting. There are many people who feel uneasy about sitting down with a roomful of strangers for a day or a week. Others simply do not want to deal with transportation, parking, findng their

14

own way, or registering for a meeting. These people are not seminar candidates. Be sure your program appeals to those who feel comfortable in the particular learning environment that you will provide.

Many public seminars can probably be marketed as a captive program. Those which are benefactor-paid have the best potential as captive programs. Salesmanship seminars serve as a good example. The program may be promoted to the general business market so as to attract independent salesmen and manufacturer's representatives, and to firms that employ salesmen, such as an insurance company or stock brokerage. In some cases, great economies of scale are afforded the seminar promoter by accommodating the general public and contract clients in the same session. This is unusual and certainly not the norm, but it is done.

Chapter 2
PROMOTION

The seminar and workshop business is a promotion-intensive one, and requires a marketing plan that can be tested and modified inexpensively. Many solid, salable programs have failed because the promoter continued to invest in marketing strategies that were clearly unprofitable, and that he would have recognized had he examined them closely.

To get the most from your promotional investment, set cost-benefit standards based upon your test-marketing experience, and cut off any avenues that do not measure up. Don't expect all of your promotions to succeed, especially if you are taking chances reaching for new business; some of your efforts will almost inevitably fail. And when they do, you'll be in good company. Some of the world's leading experts in marketing -- corporations like Heinz, Ford Motor Company and Proctor and Gamble -- have all had dismal advertising failures at one time or another. There's nothing wrong with taking a chance on one promotion as long as you have spread the risk by promoting several different ways through several different channels. In this way a seminar will not be doomed to failure if one ad, brochure, or commercial fails to attract participants.

Typically, two-thirds of your total seminar costs are for marketing. These are incurred while trying to exercise a positive influence on people's decision of whether or not to attend your program. They include promotional design, copywriting, telephone marketing, individualized selling costs, mailing expense, etc. The remaining one-third includes development costs, instructor and material costs, facilities expense, etc. Since promotional dollars must be spent in advance with no guarantees of effectiveness, thorough advance planning is necessary. This planning should include: a complete understanding of your promotional options, an exploration of mailing lists and available media, identification of your target population, and a determination of what the motivation is to attend your program.

Promotional focusing. The most successful seminar marketers have mastered an important marketing reality: the media are the markets. They begin their quest for a viable, profitable seminar, not with an interesting or needed subject, but with an identifiable and reachable audience. They find a group (market) which is easy to reach at reasonable cost. They then decide what seminar or workshop would be of sufficient interest to the market identified to produce a profitable seminar. Markets become media. The market thus is defined as the particular mailing lists, the specific publications, etc.

Promotional options. Seminars and workshops tend to be promoted in one or more of four basic models. These models are all used with varying degrees of success, although some programs will be better suited to one type of promotion by their very nature.
1. The one-step promotional model is almost always used for contract or captive training programs. The promoter has one chance to convince a prospective client that his program is needed. If the prospective client remains unmoved, the promoter tries someone else. In order for this method to generate contracts, the promoter must identify the needs of the organization, either alone or with the client's help. He must then market his program by showing that it will help to solve whatever problem is plaguing the organization at the moment. At this stage, a promoter outlines the costs and benefits of the program and attempts to elicit the prospective client's support in the form of a contract. A direct-mail brochure or a space ad in a newspaper or magazine typifies the one-step promotional model for both public and organizational seminars. It means that the promoter has only one chance to tell his story
2. The two-step (multi-step) promotional cycle is just like the one-step cycle except that it involves one or more repetitions. It might be a brochure followed up by a second mailing or two ads -- where the reader sees both. Seminar promoters often want to know whether a follow-up promotion is an effective use of their

17

marketing dollars. Generally speaking, a repeat mailing of the same promotional piece to precisely the same mailing list produces a yield which is equal to 38% to 59% of the sales obtained from the first mailing.

3. The <u>pre-sale/sale technique</u> is commonly used in investment and real-estate seminars and workshops open to the general public. The public is first invited to attend a free lecture. If the topic is interesting and the program is offered at a convenient time, people will be drawn to it. At the lecture they get an intensive sales pitch to sign up for the seminar or workshop. There are two key elements in making this method work. The first is the ability of the presenters to sell effectively at the free session. Many programs that use this type of promotion hire professionals to conduct this free session. These dynamic speakers are expert in creating an atmosphere of motivation designed to turn mildly curious onlookers into participants willing to invest time and money in a longer - program. Whether or not this option is suitable for a program is often a matter of the presenter's person- Many presenters in the seminar business are not the most adept salespeople. They are not comfortable in a role they perceive as "hucksterish," and prefer to appeal to people in a rational, sophisticated way. Since the choice to invest in continuing education is an emotional as well as rational decision, these presenters will often have difficulty in closing a sale by convincing attendees to sign up for a longer program. Promoters who are not forceful speakers can either abandon this technique as a promotional strategy or hire experts who are professional closers to make the presentation. The second necessary element for success with this two-step strategy depends upon the nature of the prospective audience. Are the people who will be drawn by a free lecture on the topic you have chosen good candidates for the longer sessions? Are they likely to be able to afford the fee? Will they be able to attend the longer program at the time you have chosen? Will an overview of the subject satisfy them or whet their appetites for more information? The topic of personal investing is a good choice for this type of promotion because it attracts those who have capital to invest and who are willing to spend some time and money to maximize their profit potential. In addition,

the complexities of the subject warrant a longer program for complete understanding. Subject, time, location, and motivation are all considerations in determining whether the pre-sale/sale technique is best for an individual program.

4. Last minute fever is the final option. "First come, first served. No advance registration. Come early if you want to get a seat." This method works with many programs, but the promoter has no way of knowing except through experience how many people will show up (if any), how large a room to rent, how many seats to set up, how much coffee to have on hand, etc. However, the very fact that it is a risk to the promoter and he has no cancellation option creates an atmosphere that is psychologically enticing to many prospects. They enjoy the "nerve" of the assumption that participants will show up, and they are curious to see if the promoter can pull it off successfully.

Promotional Strategies

Keep the offer simple and direct. If a promotional piece is too complicated or offers too many options, your prospective participants will become confused and simply ignore it. There is very little time to grab someone's attention, and if it looks like too much bother to figure out exactly what the offer is, the ad or brochure won't even get read. Discount schedules, group rates and registration deadlines create the risk of overwhelming the potential particiapnt as well as complicating the promoter's task with extra administrative details. Some of that complexity is necessary to appeal to the many ways people are likely to make a decision to come to a seminar or workshop, but there is a point of diminishing returns in providing these options. In general, the more straightforward the offer, the better it is for the promoter and the potential participant.

If you are planning to develop and promote your own seminar, you should be particularly alert to the hazards of complicating your promotional appeals. People who are capable of designing and conducting seminars are usually rather intelligent and sophisticated, and can handle complex thinking. They have the ability to simultaneously consider several variables and make complex decisions; they also have a tendency to view others as being able to do the same. Thus they structure complex and sophisticated promo-

19

tional offers which are incomprehensible to prospective participants. Professional promoters -- those who promote others' programs -- have learned to avoid this pitfall. Their experience has taught them the KISS principle: Keep It Simple, Stupid. It is helpful to give a potential participant an inducement to register immediately, but leaves the door open for last-minute decisions as well. "Act now and get a bonus. Save money before you put this brochure down. But, if you forget it today, don't worry. You can still attend at a slightly higher price." This message bespeaks the pre/sale technique. The teaser doesn't have to be a big incentive. A 10% discount or a free gift will usually be effective. With this method it is possible to minimize your risk by retaining the option to cancel a session and return the money of those who pre-registered, if the number of pre-registrations is insufficient. If early response is poor, a promoter may choose not to gamble on last-minute deciders.

A look at the media: Which is best for you?

Your promotions must work for you in a cost-effective way. How do you choose where to spend your money? First, let's look at the options:

1. Direct Mail Marketing. This is the most frequently used advertising medium in the seminar and workshop business since it's inherent advantage is the ability to target your promotion to a specific population that is most likely to be interested in your program.
2. Newspaper Advertising: This is an effective way to advertise when a) the target population is not a readily identifiable one and can't be reached by direct mail and/or b) the topic is of extremely broad interest.
3. Journals and Magazines: There are two types of magazines in which a promoter may choose to advertise --- consumer magazines (general interest publications) and trade publications for special interest groups. By thoroughly understanding the readership and distribution of a magazine a target population can be identified by region or interests, so that, although the cost per reader may be high, a large percentage of the readers will be good prospects for your program.
4. Television and Radio: Very few seminars and workshops are advertised in the electronic media in part due to

the high cost of having commercials professionally produced (a necessity in television and advisable in radio) and the often high cost of buying air time. Many promoters regard the 30 or 60 second commercial as an insufficient amount of time to communicate all of the information required to motivate someone to attend a seminar or workshop. As television becomes more specialized and segmented via cable, the cost of reaching a specialty market will decline. Some seminar promoters have had significant success using "simulated" talk-show advertising specials, particularly on TV. Such shows often feature the seminar leader as the supposed talk-show guest. Some cable operators and local stations will sell their time for such advertising programs, particularly during the late-night hours.

5. Telephone Marketing: This works well with the business community and sophisticated "upwardly mobile" groups, particularly when it is used to pre-screen interest for subsequent direct mail, to follow up or reinforce prior promotion, and/or the program deals with personal rather than professional interests. The high cost of telephone maraketing generally requires a fairly extensive seminar to be a profitable promotional device.

6. Public Relations and the Help of Others: Good public relations can be far more effective than paid advertising. There are many ways to enhance your credibility through free and low-cost channels that will increase your exposure and help spur word-of-mouth referrals. This is the best publicity there is. But bear in mind that publicity will never suffice alone; it is to be used as an adjunct to paid promotion.

7. Direct Selling: Salespeople travelling to homes or businesses trying to sell a program works best for long-term courses of several weeks' duration.

Direct-Mail Marketing

Although direct-mail marketing costs more per contact than any other kind of advertising, the individuals you reach through it have characteristics, carefully selected by you, that mark them as likely participants in your program. Unlike mass media, advertisers need pay only for those to see their ad who are likely to be interested in its content. Direct mail is most effective when the target population can be readily identified in some way: occupation, common interest, income level, trade, profession,

21

licensing, academic degree, income level, etc. Mailing lists are available that characterize the human animal by every conceivable variation and permutation. There are subscriber lists, such as those who subscribe to "Business Week" magazine; buyer lists, such as those who spent more than $20 on training materials in the past year; people with common characteristics, such as scientists, listed by discipline; or business executives, such as those in the foundry field. Whomever you want to reach, it can be done through direct mail.

Once you've identified the characteristics of your likely participants, an invaluable reference for selecting mailing lists is "Direct Mail Lists Rates & Data," Standard Rates & Data Service, 3004 Glenview Road, Wilmette, IL 60091. This publication provides information on over 40,000 direct mail marketing lists that can be rented or bought in the United States and Canada. For each list, the following information is provided:

1. Whom to contact to buy or rent the list.
2. Description of criteria for inclusion on the list.
3. List Sources.
4. Rental rates, by quantity.
5. Minimum number of names that must be rented.
6. Method of addressing labels.
7. Frequency of updates and list maintenance.
8. Other information relevant to a particular list.

A 20% discount on the rental price can be realized by buying or renting lists as a mailing list broker. The discount is usually available to advertising agencies, too. This commission can be earned by establishing your own list brokerage or ad agency operation (see chapter three).

The mailing list is regarded by most promoters as being the most crucial element in the success of a promotion. Great care and caution should be taken in the selection of a list. Professional assistance from mailing list brokers or direct-marketing consultants is often well advised.

Your direct mail piece should be in the hands of the prospective participant sufficiently in advance of the program date to maximize attendance; a minimum of three weeks for local programs, four weeks if they are expected to travel a short distance, and six weeks if it would be a lengthy trip. If you are promoting to people who are likely to have a very heavy schedule and commitments, such as medical doctors, then the promotion should reach them eight, ten or even twelve weeks in advance, and perhaps with a reminder sent out later. If you are mailing by bulk rate (third class) which is usually the least expensive, the length of time which the Postal Service will require to deliver your mailing piece is uncertain. Depending upon the time of year, the volume of mail being handled, the distance the mailing piece must go, and the Post Office from which it is mailed, delivery may take anywhere from a few days to several weeks. Direct mail service organizations (letter shops) can often give you "guesstimates" that are fairly reliable.

The expected rate of return from a direct mail promotion for a seminar will range from 1/10 of 1% to 3% of the entire mailing. Most promoters consider one half of one percent as a good rate of response. There is a great number of variables which will influence the rate of response, not the least of which is the price of the seminar. Concentration on "capture ratios" for direct mail response is not advised. Some promoters, selling $400 -$700 seiminars, for example, find that 1/10 of 1% is satisfactory to produce acceptable profits.; others who sell $50 - $150 seminars find that 8/10 of 1% to 1-1/2% is necessary to stay in business. You are better off to think in terms of the ratio between dollars invested in promotion and marketing compared to dollars of registration fees earned. If registration fees are three times your marketing costs (a ratio of 3:1) you will probably have a profitable operation, given normal expense levels for conducting seminars.

The conventional wisdom of direct mail holds that a test mailing should contain no fewer than 3,000 to 5,000 names to avoid statistical aberration. But using 500-1000 names will often provide a reasonably satisfactory test of the market, and the money saved by a small mailing can be used to enable you to test more mailing lists or promotions, in case one of them doesn't pull for you.

When a seminar being promoted is of value and interest to both the employer and employee, should you promote to the prospective participants' superiors or the training or personnel department, or just to the individuals who would ultimately attend? There are no hard and fast rules on this, since every seminar company is different and each is distintive. Promotions should be evaluated on a case-by-case basis. You might want to reach both, since one will make the buying decision, but the other has some influence (albeit less), too.

Newspaper and Magazine Advertising

These can be two of the most cost-effective ways to promote, if you understand the economics of the media and the demographics of their readerships. In the United States there are four publications, which together provide a complete market picture of the print media. They are:

1. Newspaper Rates & Data
2. Consumer Magazine & Farm Publication Rates & Data
3. Business Publications Rates & Data
4. Newspaper Circulation Analysis

They are all published by Standard Rate & Data Service, 3004 Glenview Road, Wilmette, IL 60091. Virtually every public library has these books in the reference section. The first three will provide you with the following information on the type of publication indexed:

1. Editorial profile
2. Representatives and their branch offices
3. Commission paid to advertising agencies
4. Advertising rates and charges
5. Deadline for submitting copy
6. Circulation
7. Ad sizes and (for newspapers) number and width of columns. Most papers accept standard advertising units. The Wall Street Journal is an exception with six columns, which means that your display will be wider.

Newspaper Circulation Analysis provides data on the readership of newspapers that will enable you to choose the best newspaper or combination of media in every metropolitan area. It includes the income level and other demographic characteristics of newspapers' readerships, listed by county, television market area, and Standard Metropolitan Statistical Area. For instance, suppose you were planning a workshop in Los Angeles. How do you choose a newspaper to advertise it? Los Angeles is a major market that behaves in unexpected ways. In most cities its size, the dominant newspaper reaches between 55% and 65% of all households. Los Angeles' dominant newspaper, The Los Angeles Times, has less than 30% household coverage in the metropolitan area. The competition comes, not from the other metropolitan daily paper as one would expect, but from the suburban dailies. The Orange County Register, The Daily (Valley) News, The Daily Breeze, The Long Beach Independent, and others have achieved significant coverage in segments of the L.A. market. Newspaper Circulation

Analysis will enable you to identify the paper that is being read in the entire locale of your program site by your most likely participants. Used in conjunction with Newspaper Rates & Data, you can identify the newspaper that will reach the greatest number of your targeted market at the lowest cost.

The New York metropolitan area is another complex and expensive market. A cursory look at the market might leave a promoter with the impression that The New York Daily News is preferable advertising-wise to The New York Times because of its higher circulation concentrated in the New York metropolitan area. However, a closer examination of the demographics of their markets reveals that the likely participants of most business and professional seminars and workshops will be reading the Times, not The News. If a promoter decided to extend his coverage beyond the Times, chances are he still wouldn't advertise in the News. His best additional media buy at this point would be be in one of the suburban dailies in New Jersey, Long Island, or Connecticut. These have readers with demographic character-istics similar to Times readers, that mark them as likely candidates for a particular kind of program.

Many national newspapers and magazines publish regional editions. It costs much less to advertise in the south-western edition of The Wall Street Journal, for example, than in the national edition; and this will provide as good a test of that publication as paying four or five times that amount. You can make the most of an ad in a regional edition by doing a seminar circuit through several cities in that region. When planning a regional circuit, however, be sure that the cities and states that you assume belong to a certain region are in fact covered by the regional edition of the publication. Remember that your midwest may not be their midwest.

Ad copy deadlines for magazines (even a regional or city edition of a national magazine) are often between eight and ten weeks prior to publication, so it helps to plan ahead. But if you don't, there is a little-known way to save money by purchasing space in magazines at the last minute. Often, a magazine's published rates are subject to negotiation about two days preceding and following the issue closing deadline. This is particularly true with some of the smaller trade, professional and business journals. If their advertising is not sold out for that issue, they may have to remove a signature (several pages), run house ads, or change some layouts. They would rather run your ad at a lower rate than not make any money at all on that space. If you can guarantee overnight delivery of camera-ready copy of your ad to them, it not only earns them money they would not otherwise have made, but also may save them considerable effort in rearranging the magazine; so they will sometimes happily accept your ad at a discounted rate. Of course, if their advertising happens to be sold out for that issue, you take the chance of not getting your ad in (but you won't pay for it either). This risk can be minimized by using other advertising avenues in conjunction with this one.

Newspapers sell four kinds of advertising: national classified, local classified, national display, and local or retail display. Whether you advertise in The London Times or the Washington Post, classified advertising is the least expensive. The classified section of a newspaper is often the least read of any section. Unless a person is seeking a job, buying or selling a car or a home, etc., he is unlikely to read the classifieds. However, those who do read it tend to read it more carefully than the typical reader who reads for news.

Since some people read the classifieds religiously — those looking for business opportunities, for real estate investments, or estate sales and auctions, for example — your ad might do very well in the classified section if your seminar is of interest to the people who regularly read the classified ads. An ad for a workshop on how to get a better job, how to write an effective resume, or how to evaluate franchise offers might work well in the classified section, but you will probably find it of value to also advertise in other sections (display ads).

The "tickler" ad, which is designed to arouse enough curiosity to provoke a follow-up call for further information, can be an effective, low-cost method of gauging readers' interest in your topic. One successful classified "tickler" ad for a seminar read simply, "Grantsmanship — How to Get Government Grants," followed by a phone number. When the number was dialed, a recorded message described the seminar, and callers were asked to leave their name and address if they wanted to receive a brochure with more information. About 80% of all callers left their names, of which 60% eventually registered for the seminar — a more than respectable response rate for an ad that cost a fraction of the price of a larger ad which would communicate

26

the complete message.

Display advertising is probably the best newspaper option for most seminars and workshops. Display ads, like classified ads, are accepted on both a national and local basis. Some newspapers have no rate differential between national and local ads, but most leading papers do. Local rates are almost always less expensive, and are intended for the retail businesses in the newspaper's delivery area. Rates are lower due to competition from radio, TV and other papers, particularly suburban and neighborhood papers. For example, it costs about two and a half times as much to advertise in the Washington Post at national rates than it does at local rates. Conversely, some papers like The San Francisco Chronicle do not permit seminars to be advertised at local rates, even if the promoter is in the local area. All of their seminar and workshop advertising is considered national. To find the local rates for a particular newspaper, either ask them to send you a local rate card or contact their representative's local office. A permanent business address in the paper's community is usually necessary to qualify for local rates, but some promoters fulfill this requirement by contracting with a local answering service and using that address to meet the conditions for the lower rate. They find that the savings are substantial in cities where there is a significant rate differential, and where they advertise frequently; this more than covers the expense of the answering service.

National advertising rates in newspapers and magazines are almost always commissionable. That is, advertising agencies receive a 15% commission on ads which they place. Sometimes, ad agencies are also entitled to an additional 2% cash discount. Local and classified rates are almost never commissionable.

To get the greatest impact from display advertising, send camera-ready copy to the newspaper or magazine, rather than letting them set the ad for you. Whether you have it professionally done or prepare it yourself, it will usually be more effective than a "pub set" ad, which the publication typesets for you, usually with minimal or no attention to design and presentation.

Certain newspapers and magazines will run your ad on a "per-inquiry" (P.I.) basis. They will insert your ad when they have space available, at no cost to you, then split the returns from that ad on a percentage basis. For example, if a seminar is advertised in a trade journal on a

27

P.I. basis, the registration fee of $150 might be sent directly to the journal from the registrant, and the journal would keep $60 and send the remaining $90 to the promoter. Although some publications have a firm policy against P.I. advertising, many will consider this type of arrangement on a case-by-case basis. They will not make it generally known that they do so, since they would prefer to let the advertiser take the full risk of an ad pulling for a product or service by simply charging their standard rates. The P.I. arrangement offers the promoter a lower rate of return but no risk, and it is often available upon inquiry.

Newspapers in a hotly competitive market may be willing to accept a lower rate for your advertising rather than lose it to their rivals. You never know until you ask!

Where to Run an Ad

Most newspapers will not guarantee placement of an ad, so you may not have much choice in the matter. They will try to honor your choice of placement, but as a small advertiser you may be "bumped" by one of their preferred customers -- someone like a cigarette company, liquor company or local department store. It is sometimes possible to purchase preferred placement for 20% to 30% over the base rate, and it may be worth the extra cost if it gets your ad onto the "right" page instead of buried in the obituaries.

Any reason that you can give the newspaper or sales representative to go out of their way for you may help get favorable placement for your ad. Develop a personal rapport with the sales representative who takes your ad. If he is remotely interested, invite him to your program free of charge. Write a letter to his boss praising the great job he is doing for you.

If, by policy or politesse, you are given a choice regarding the position of your ad, here are your options:
1. Main news. Most people read it. You'll rarely go wrong.
2. Sports. O.K. if appealing to a male audience.
3. Lifestyle. O.K. if appealing to a female audience.
4. Business. Good, if your program is expensive or appeals to those with a high income.

The more often you run your ads and the bigger they are, the more people you will attract. This is a pretty basic rule-of-thumb, but there is a point of diminishing returns, a break-even point that can only be determined for a particular program by testing various combinations. For many programs, running an ad four to six days in advance of your program in the daily media and eight to nine days in the national media is sufficient to attract interested readers. In other cases, several weeks of lead time will be necessary to produce the highest response.

Best Times to Advertise

In the Fall of 1986, I surveyed 415 seminar and workshop developers and promoters about their experiences in conducting programs throughout the country. Of these, 239 responded. Their opinions of the best times to advertise a seminar or workshop follows:

Best days of the week.

Newspapers	Radio
1. Sunday	1. Monday
2. Tuesday	2. Wednesday
3. Wednesday	3. Tuesday
4. Monday	4. Thursday
5. Thursday	5. Friday
6. Saturday	6. Sunday
7. Friday	7. Saturday

Best months of the year to advertise in magazines

1. September	7. May
2. January	8. December
3. March	9. June
4. October	10. November
5. April	11. August
6. February	12. July

Setting up Your Own Agency

You may wonder why anyone trying to launch a seminar or workshop would want to go to the trouble and expense of setting up his own advertising agency. The reason is simple: considerable savings can be realized on your advertising costs for surprisingly little trouble and expense. Almost all media pay commissions to advertising agencies, brokers or representatives. Print media pay a 15% commission on their national advertising rates, and about a third of the newspapers and magazines also have a 2% cash discount which is accorded only to advertising agencies. By establishing your own agency, your up-front savings represents 15%-17% of the total cost. This savings extends to other types of advertising costs as well -- for example, 20% on the rental of mailing lists.

The main requirement for setting up an advertising agency is simply to have the nerve to do it. It is unlikely that anyone will challenge your right to become an ad agency executive. The procedure is simple:

1. Select a name. It should be different from the name of your other business.
2. File the name with your state if required.
3. Open a checking account in that name. Always write checks for advertising expenses on this account.

You are in business. If you choose, you can serve outside clients as well to add to your credibility and prestige as an advertising agency, and to help get those media discounts.

One pitfall that many promoters succumb to at this stage is that of overextending credit to pay for advertising expenses. Don't expect your receipts from a program to pay for its advertising expenses if it means spending money you don't have. Heavy advertising does not always guarantee a large turnout, and if a program does not meet your expectations of profitability, as sometimes happens, a substantial advertising debt and no profits will result. If you spend only available money on promotion, you'll get just as good a test, and have enough money to run that program again.

Now that you have created an advertising agency, deal with media representatives and media agencies whenever possible, instead of placing your ads directly with a newspaper, magaazine, TV or radio station. About 85% to 88% of all newspapers, and most magazines have representatives in major cities who work on a commission or fee basis. Since they profit from your advertising, they will be less inclined to challenge your right to take an agency commission.

There are some publications that are diffficult to get your ad into, much less earn a commission on. There is such a high demand for their advertising space that they simply don't have to lower their rates for anyone, much less pay a commission to anyone they feel isn't entitled to it. If you build up a media group that pays you an agency commission, it becomes difficult for them to reject you.

Chapter 3
PROMOTIONAL STRATEGY

Designing Your Promotion

The first consideration in promotional design must be getting your message read. Obtaining the reader's attention is not easy and warrants your serious effort and creativity.

When your brochure reaches your prospects through the mail, your first task is to get them to open the envelope — or the self-mailer, which is used in most seminar promotions. A busy business executive receives between 90 and 110 direct-mail promotional pieces a week at home and at work. Only a minority get opened, much less read. Your promotion must stand out in the crowd. A catchy headline, distinctive graphics or odd-size pieces are techniques often used by promoters to capture the reader's attention.

Ask yourself these questions: Does my brochure or advertisement capture and sustain the reader's attention? Is the first thing the eye automatically rests on in the ad the most important benefit? Does it lead the reader's eye to the next most important feature, and have him immersed in my message before he quite knows why? The graphic design of the piece should control and direct the reader's attention.

Identify the benefits of the program to the reader and make the most of them. People respond on an emotional as well as rational level, so your promotion must provide a motivational message as well as a logical one. Describe the information or advantages they will garner from your program — how they will change, what they will be able to do and what they will learn. If the advantages of participation are also part of the motivational message, don't hesitate to say it twice; repetition is marvelous in promotional brochures. You cannot say good things too often.

Be reader-centered and benefit-oriented in your ad copy. If your promotion launches into a minute description of the seminar or workshop before answering the reader's implicit question, "What can this do for me?" then you have already lost him. Keep the language clear and specific, bearing in mind that, although you may be intimately familiar with the concepts of your program and the ad copy before it leaves your hands, it must "come across" to the casual reader in one reading.

A good promotion is visually appealing and enlightening. A liberal sprinkling of photographs and drawings can be informative as well as reassuring. A picture of you (if you're good looking), product shots of your seminar materials, classroom scenes -- all these will help make the program more concrete, more real, in the mind of the reader. Ours is a visually oriented society, and many people will get more information from the styling and graphics of your ad than from the text, so be sure they convey the same message and image as your copy. We are trained from first grade on to read the words under the picture first. Use the caption space under the pictures to give your strongest promotional messages and to detail benefits. Don't make the mistake of assuming that you are required to explain the contents of the picture, which are probably obvious anyway.

When preparing your promotion, consider buying outside expert services when absolutely necessary. Printing, graphics, and advertising are very price-sensitive fields, so it pays to shop around. When your program is thriving, you won't mind spending more to have your promotions professionally produced, but during the testing stage, every nickel counts. Having your ad designed by professionals can be very expensive, but often the results are worth it. To cut down or eliminate this expense and still have a sophisticated ad, you can learn how to do your own graphics and paste-up. A course in graphic design at your local community college will more than pay for itself in the savings you will realize by being able to use a T-square to do some simple paste-up copy and illustrations. There are ways to produce professional looking ad pieces at a fraction of the cost of buying them on the open market. For example, typewritten material can be made to look typeset by preparing your copy with a distinctive typeface and justified right-hand margins; and then having it photo-reduced. Most print shops will do this at a cost of about a dollar a page. Of course, if you have a personal computer and printer, you can approximate the work of most print shops at no cost at all.

The size and color of a brochure are two variables that are productive to experiment with. In some cases, the smaller the brochure the better, because it's less costly to produce and easier for people to read and keep. In other cases, a larger brochure is necessary to build credibility and interest. Sometimes the promotional message is too sophisticated or complex to fit into a small brochure, and requires a larger format. The color of your brochure should be well integrated into the overall design of the piece. Reader response to the elements of size and color is difficult to measure, so follow your own tastes and instincts. Test different sizes and colors to see which produces the best response. If you come across a combination that works particularly well for you, stick with it, but continue to test different options from time to time.

Testimonials. The response to testimonials in your brochure will vary, depending on your audience. Some people will either not believe them or not care what others think, so they won't be particularly responsive. Conversely, testimonials can help your credibility with someone who is hesitating to register because he's never heard of you before and isn't much of a risk-taker. If you show him that others in his situation have found your program worthwhile, he might decide to take that risk. If you choose to try testimonials, they should be strong ones -- nothing vague or open to varying interpretations. Testimonials are perhaps best acquired through the program evaluation that participants are asked to fill out at the end of each session. When you receive some comments that you would like to use as promotional testimonials, write that individual a letter thanking him for his responses and asking for permission to use it in your marketing copy. Make it easy for him to respond by providing a permission form and a stamped, self-addressed envelope.

Include a line in your brochure or ad inviting people to come to your office and actually read the original comments. This not only adds to their credibility, but is a legal requirement in some areas.

Names of famous people or organizations that have attended your program can be a worthwhile addition to your brochure or ad, particularly if you are not well known but some of your participants are. They add an element of reassurance to potential but indecisive participants. It is advisable to have the written permission of past clients before using their names in any promotion.

Checklist for Promotional Design Your marketing piece should contain the following information:
1. Motivational message. Point out the advantages and benefits of participation.
2. Cost, registration and payment procedure. Include the credit cards you'll accept and your policy on checks and purchase orders.
3. Your address and phone number. Very basic, but often forgotten (or put solely on the business reply card), which can be very disconcerting to the prospect who receives a brochure second-hand without a reply card.
4. Seminar presenters. Background information and credentials. Perhaps pictures.
5. Seminar materials. Describe the information and format in which it is presented. Include product shots if your materials are handsomely packaged.
6. What they should do if they can't attend. Can they attend a later program, or buy the seminar materials? Give them some options.
7. Business reply mechanism. A phone (toll-free?) number to call, a business reply card -- some way to make response to your program easy. More than one way is better.
8. An "Act Now" kicker. A reason to respond to your promotion before putting down the brochure, newspaper or magazine, and forgetting about it.
9. Endorsements, sponsors, testimonials, or any other kind of accreditation. Reputable backing from recognized individuals and organizations will add credibility and make your program seem less of a risk to potential participants.
10. Tax-deductible status (where and when applicable). The standard language for this is "An income tax deduction may be allowed for educational expenses undertaken to maintain or improve professional skills. This includes

registration, travel, meals, lodging. At this writing the full impact of the Tax Reform Act of 1987 on the deductibility of seminar fees remains somewhat uncertain and quite open to interpretation. The following information was provided to the readers of my newsletter, "The Professional Consultant & Seminar Business Report," October 1986:

Marketers who have benefited by providing notice to prospective participants that the fee for their seminars and workshops is a tax-deductible expense, will have to adjust their marketing strategy. The new law specifies that individuals will have to expend $1,000 on such educational expenses for purposes of professional development before taking a deduction on further expenditures. And, the tax benefit for expense beyond the first $1,000 will be a function of the tax bracket. under the old code, expenses for continuing professional development education to include registration fees, materials, travel and related items were fully deductible. Since corporations will still be able to deduct the expense on behalf of their employees, the only real impact will be on individuals who are spending their own money for programs. Individuals who are incorporated for purposes of doing business will also likely not be impacted. Non-incorporated individuals account for approximately 11% of total public seminar and workshop revenues. Hardest hit by the new provision will be colleges and universities, store-front educational operations and school districts. While seminar companies obtain only 7% of total revenues from the personal funds of non-incorporated individuals, the education market obtains approximately 47% of gross from this source.

11. Cancellation policy. If you retain the option to canccel, specify this in your promo. The following standard wording is often used: "If enrollment is insufficient in this program, participants will be notified no later than [date]," or "All dates and locations subject to cancellation on prior written notice to enrolled participants." Include your policy on participant cancellation, which usually takes the form of a cut-off date for cancellation with a full refund, and perhaps a partial refund or application of the fee to other services after the cut-off date.
12. Contact for further information. Provide a name, phone

number, or address to encourage people to contact you with any questions or for further information. Since it may be useful to the reader to see these advisory suggestions in example form, you may wish to review a brochure for my own seminars which appear on the following pages (in reduced size).

Making Response to Your Promotion Easy. People should be able to register for your program with minimal effort, and in the case of consumer-oriented programs, at no cost to themselves for doing so. There are several ways to facilitate this:

1. The toll-free call. This is the most convenient reply mechanism for your registrants. All they have to do is dial a number, say "I'll be there. Charge it to my credit card -- here's the number," and they are registered. Check your telephone company to determine the procedures and rates for such services. You can save money on toll-free calls by sharing a line with others through the many companies set up for this purpose. They can be located through advertisements in business publications or in the yellow pages of your phone book listed under "answering services." Your brochure or ad directs a caller to ask for a department or code number so that when someone calls, an operator takes his reservation, with nothing to indicate to the caller that it is not your own office. A typical charge for this service is $2.50 per reservation and $1.50 for an inquiry.
2. Collect calls. Not many people will take you up on collect calls, so it's often cheaper than a toll-free set-up. Just the fact that it is offered however tells people that you want their business enough to be accommodating. It will also garner reservations from those who would simply not register if they had to pay for the call.
3. Business-Reply Mail. Enclosing a postage-paid, self-addressed envelope or reply card with your brochure is now one of the most widely-used response mechanisms. You could gamble that an interested person will find an envelope, stamp and address it (properly) himself, but why make him work?. If you want that extra business "go the extra mile." Instead, provide an envelope with a spot for a stamp that says "Place stamp here.The Post Office will not deliver mail without postage."

Whenever you are mailing to business and professional

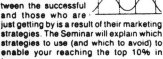

THE SEMINAR ON SEMINARS

NEW MARKETING TECHNIQUES FOR SEMINARS & WORKSHOPS

DEVELOPED & CONDUCTED BY

HOWARD L. SHENSON

SAN FRANCISCO

Wednesday & Thursday
October 29th & 30th
9:00 AM until 4:30 PM
Westin St. Francis Hotel
Union Square

NEW YORK CITY

Wednesday & Thursday
December 3rd & 4th
9:00 AM until 4:30 PM
Marriott Marquis
1535 Broadway

LOS ANGELES

Thursday & Friday
February 5th & 6th
9:00 AM until 4:30 PM
Hyatt at L.A. Airport
6225 W. Century Blvd.

CHICAGO

Wednesday & Thursday
April 8th & 9th
9:00 AM until 4:30 PM
Mayfair Regent Hotel
181 East Lakeshore Dr.

An Important Message:
FACTS VS. OPINIONS

This Seminar is based upon disciplined research and factual data, not hunches or limited experience. While there is always a place for taste and opinion, they are no substitute for hard data on what works, doesn't work and why!

Recently, I was invited to speak at an important technical conference for professionals in the seminar business. Usually when I speak at a conference, I fly in just prior to my talk and depart immediately upon its conclusion. Because this meeting was billed as having so many highly informed, prominent speakers, I elected to attend the entire conference with the hope of learning a great deal. To my surprise, I learned little.

I was appalled to witness the conference participants, myself included, receiving a great deal of erroneous information from allegedly credible sources. I saw speakers make dogmatic statements which research evidence indicates are simply not true. I observed the time of highly sophisticated people being wasted on unimportant, even trivial, concerns. This is unacceptable and shocking!

Enlightened opinions may have been acceptable a few years ago, but they are no longer sufficient. This business is now far too sophisticated and the risks in being wrong are too costly.

I deal mostly in the world of facts. The research which I do for my newsletter, my work with clients, the experience of marketing my own seminars and the communications which I have with other successful seminar providers has resulted in my being able to collect vast quantities of reliable data on seminar promotion. We no longer have to guess! In most cases we know what works!

This Seminar is based on carefully tested, factual data. Opinions are important. They are a part of this Seminar, but they are clearly labeled as such and are considered within a context of what is known to be true.

—*Howard L. Shenson*

HOWARD L. SHENSON
20750 Ventura Boulevard, Suite 206, Woodland Hills, California 91364
818/703-1415

© 1986. Howard L. Shenson

PERFORMAX

Performax Systems
International, Inc
12755 State Highway 55
Minneapolis, MN 55441
612 559-6327
©1986, Howard L. Shenson

WHAT YOU WILL LEARN

Successful Direct Mail Marketing Strategies

What works/doesn't work and why

14 strategies to increase direct mail response

How far in advance to mail—research data

How many brochures to mail—profit planning model

How often to mail and a precise follow-up mailing strategy

When to use catalogs vs. brochures—factual evidence

Improving direct mail pieces—color, paper, pictures, size, etc.

Brochure design—a working clinic and examples of highly successful promotional brochures

Best months of the year to send out direct mail—research data

Effective Advertising Campaigns

When to use newspapers, magazines, radio and television to promote a seminar or workshop

How to select and buy advertising media

How to design ads which produce results

Best days of the week, months of the year to advertise—research results

Best sizes, locations, frequencies for ads—factual data

Tickler ads, zone ads and other strategies for high yield on a limited promotional budget

Powerful Copy Writing Techniques

What to say/not say in your promotional copy

11 Strategies for improving already good copy

Analyzing copy choice—a working clinic

Testing promotional copy—a model and specific tactics

Examples of well-written, highly successful seminar promotion copy

How to distinguish your seminar from the competition

Creative Promotional Strategies

How to use free lectures/seminars to sell seminars

How to increase telephone registrations

Using credit cards, even for corporate paid seminars, to increase registrations by 11.2-21.6% and improve cash flow, advance registrations

Utilizing The Concentric Circle Theory of Seminar Promotion to increase promotional yield by 14.7-26.5%

How to structure payment options to increase registration by 9.4-18.2%

Discounts and premiums as a strategy to increase registrations—what works/doesn't work and why

How to design a refund/cancellation policy that maximizes profit potential

Enlightened Mailing List Selection & Testing

How to identify high response lists before renting

How to create even higher yields from already successful lists

Why you should stop paying attention to capture rates

How to do a list test for less than $450 in total expense, even when the minimum list rental is 3,000 names

How to improve response rate from marginal lists

How to obtain discounts on lists

How to select a mailing list broker

Definite Test Marketing Strategies

Selecting seminar/workshop topics—A highly reliable, field tested model to insure success

How to test any seminar for less than $900

Perfect A/B Splits, Matched pairs, Nth Name, Zip Numeral Tests—specific field testing models

When to use market testing, market research, competitive research

How to definitely test alternative fees/prices without incurring the wrath of participants

Testing premiums and discounts

Best test markets—research results

Setting The Best Fee/Price For Your Program

Price testing models

Research results on impact of changing fees for an existing program

Profit Planning and Risk Analysis—a model

Psychological pricing and pricing barriers —what are they and how to deal with them

Seminar price sensitivity to business cycle—how to predict and respond

Preparing for the next recession—specific promotional strategies for survival and profitability based on research

Bundling and unbundling—when to use

SEMINAR MATERIALS

I will be providing you with a truly extensive set of seminar materials—more than 200 pages. Some of the materials will be used in the Seminar, but much is intended for your continuing study after the Seminar. The materials are practical and strategic and contain examples, samples, forms, checklists, models and systems.

Marketing & Management Enhancements To Increase Profits

Predictive model for determining promotional results, cash flow and profitability.

How to develop a successful back-of-the-room and after-seminar selling system

11 high profit at-seminar/after-seminar products and services to sell

Soft-sell strategies which increase profits and don't offend participants

Most profitable cities in which to conduct seminars—research data and a system to insure success in location selection

Crucial market research data to collect from participants to make your next promotion more profitable

How to sell consulting services to seminar participants

How to boost seminar registrations through low-cost/no-cost public relations

Specific techniques for increasing "word of mouth" referrals and sales

Co-Op Promotion Strategies

How to encourage others to promote your program for free or at low cost

The Cost & Expense Side of Seminars

Strategies to reduce hotel/conference facility rental cost by 13.4-35.6%

How to buy coffee, food, other hospitality services at 1.3-29.2% savings

How to reduce printing costs by 9.1-39.6%

How to start your own advertising agency/direct-mail brokerage to reduce promotion expense by 16.8-19.3%

Facilities/services checklist and set-up instructions which insures you get what you want at the prices you expect

How to negotiate for room blocks

Strategies for reducing the negative impact of bad paper and uncollectables

AT THE SEMINAR YOU WILL RECEIVE

Sample brochures and ads for successful seminars

Seminar Topic Evaluation Matrix

Most Profitable Seminar Cities Selection Tool

Promotional Yield/Program Profitability Predictive Model

Comprehensive Marketing Plan For Your Seminar

Facilities Set-Up Instruction Form & Checklist

Promotional Brochure and/or Advertisement For Your Seminar—ready to go to typesetter

The Seminar Registration & Tracking System

And much, much more.

HOWARD L. SHENSON
20750 Ventura Boulevard, Suite 206, Woodland Hills, California 91364
818/703-1415

THE SEMINAR APPROACH & LEARNING METHOD

This is a working seminar. Don't expect to show up, take a few notes and leave relaxed. Participants in my seminars usually leave exhausted. You will be worked hard, every minute, and you will even have homework at night. Here's why!

Your time and money is of great value. First, there is the Seminar fee. It is not insubstantial. I make no apologies. In this life you get what you pay for. Second, there is the cost of travel. Third, and most important, is the value of your time. Your time is of significant value. If it isn't, you shouldn't attend this Seminar.

My philosophy in business is to give your customers and clients at least twice what they expect. This keeps them happy and saying nice things about you. Hence, I am compelled to make the value of attending this Seminar worth many thousands of dollars.

The Seminar is hands-on. Not only will you master a vast quantity of proven, state-of-the-art strategy on the marketing of seminars and workshops; you will leave the seminar with hard, tangible products, outcomes and results. Be prepared to work.

I feel this is an outstanding opportunity for you to produce truly meaningful results for your seminars and workshops. Bring your ideas and you will be provided with the time and professional assistance to leave with:

• A fully developed promotional brochure and/or advertisement which is ready to go to the typesetter.

• A complete marketing plan. You will know when to promote, how to promote, what lists to use/how many pieces to mail or what media to use and when.

• A complete follow-up promotional plan. Specific step-by-step strategies you can follow to do follow-up promotion and increase yield and profits.

• A test-marketing plan. You will develop precise strategies to test your seminar for less than $900.

• The fee (price) for your program having been set.

We can work on a new program or we can tear apart and remodel the marketing for one of your existing programs. You work and produce hard outcomes while you learn. It's the best way.

EARLY REGISTRATION BONUS

The first 12 individuals to register and pay for each Seminar will receive as a gift a one-year subscription to my monthly newsletter. **The Professional Consultant & Seminar Business Report** (value $96). Current subscribers will receive a one-year extension.

ABOUT THE SEMINAR LEADER

To make an intelligent decision about attending this Seminar you should evaluate my background and experience to conduct the program. The following information is designed to assist you in this task.

In the last 18 years I have designed, developed, marketed and managed in excess of

Howard L. Shenson

175,000 participant days of training. I conduct my own proprietary seminars and have served as a consultant on seminar promotion to more than 100 clients, including Fortune 100 companies, universities, non-profits, medium size firms and entrepreneurs.

I am the editor/publisher of **The Professional Consulting and Seminar Business Report**, a monthly newsletter on seminar and workshop marketing. I have written and had published 18 different books and audio cassette learning packages including **How To Create & Market A Successful Seminar or Workshop** and **How To Develop & Promote Profitable Seminars & Workshops**.

Prior to entering full-time, professional consulting and the seminar business, I served in administrative and teaching positions with the University of Southern California and California State University. I received my bachelor's degree from Seattle University of Washington.

(continued on Back Page)

SEMINAR FEE

The fee for the seminar is $495 and includes all seminar materials, refreshments breaks and follow on assistance.

HOW TO REGISTER

There are two ways to register. 1) Complete the registration form provided in this brochure and mail. 2) Telephone your registration and charge to your American Express, VISA or MasterCard. Phone 612/559-6327

Space is strictly limited to insure maximum learning. Registration will be accepted in the order received.

A confirmation will be mailed to you upon receipt of your registration.

TAX DEDUCTION CONTINUING EDUCATION CREDIT

U.S. Treasury Regulation 1.162-5 permits an income tax deduction for educational expenses (registration fees and cost of travel, meals and lodging) undertaken to maintain or improve skills required in one's employment, trade or business. This course is normally accepted for 1.4 CEU's.

CANCELLATIONS

You may cancel your registration at any time up to 72 hours prior to the start of the Seminar and receive a full refund. Cancellations received after this time will result in full credit which may be used for any future seminar or publication purchase. You may, of course, substitute another to attend in your place without additional charge.

SLEEPING ROOMS

Sleeping rooms have been blocked at each Seminar hotel. You will receive full details upon receipt of registration.

QUESTIONS?

Call Performax at 612/559-6327 or speak with Howard Shenson, the seminar developer/leader directly. 818/703-1415.

Seminars & Workshops

TAKE ACTION...

You will leave this course with an action plan you can put to work the very next day. You will know how to select seminar topics which sell, how to promote your program, what fee to charge, and how to plan, manage and control all strategic activities necessary for a successful and profitable seminar or workshop.

And, you will leave this course with finished brochures and advertisements ready to go to the typesetter/printer as well as a completed marketing and test-market plan.

ABOUT THE SEMINAR LEADER, CONT.

I have been fortunate to gain considerable exposure through articles which I have written for trade, business and professional publications, frequent speaking engagements at national professional association meetings and conferences, and through more than 200 appearances on radio and TV talk and news shows as well as more than 400 interview and news articles which have been published in magazines and newspapers.

I engage in regular and substantial research about the seminar and workshop business and will share the results of my research with you generously.

CALL ME BEFORE & AFTER THE SEMINAR

If you have any questions about the content of this Seminar or its suitability for your purposes, please don't hesitate to call me for a frank discussion at 818/703-1415.

Your Seminar doesn't end at 4:30 on the second day. Call me after the Seminar, as often as you like. I will be happy to answer your questions or refer you to an information source which may have the answers you need.

Howard L. Shenson

PERFORMAX

Performax Systems
International, Inc.
2755 State Highway 55
Minneapolis, MN 55441

HOWARD L. SHENSON
20750 Ventura Boulevard, Suite 206, Woodland Hills, California 91364
818/703-1415

people at their offices where they have stamps and post-tage meters, you can probably get away without paying the return postage. A business reply envelope and order registration form, rather than a business reply card, should be sent if you expect people to enclose a check.

4. <u>At-The-Door Registration.</u> Some people don't get them-selves organized in time to pre-register, or simply for-get to do so. They may decide to take a chance on get-ting in on the day of the program, and you can help by permitting them that option. Say in your advertisement, "Unable to register in advance? A few seats will be set aside for those unable to pre-register. See you at the Seminar!" This implies that they may not gain admit-tance if they don't pre-register, but it leaves that op-tion open for last-minute deciders who are willing to take the risk.

5. <u>Discounts for Early Registration.</u> An inducement to pre-register, such as a free gift or price reduction, will spur those early registrations and give people a reason to act immediately. This, in turn, will reduce some of your risk and allow you to make more accurate prepara-tions regarding the size of the room, refreshments, etc

6. <u>Credit Cards.</u> Mastercard, Visa, and American Express are the cards most commonly used. If your program ap-peals to the general public, accepting credit cards will increase your enrollment by 20% or more. There are representatives at banks in your area who can set you up as an authorized agent for accepting credit cards. This slightly increases your expense (by about 5%), but the additional business will make this cost more than worthwhile. The costs of handling credit cards are:
    -An initial enrollment or membership charge, usually about $25.
    -Charge card machine. About $25.
    -The transaction charge. This can be anywhere from 1-7/8% to 5-1/2%, depending on the volume of business you do and the bank you are dealing with. The rate may vary from bank to bank, so it pays to shop around for the best deal. You may have to pay a high rate initially, but it can be renegotiated downward as your volume increases.

7 <u>Discounts for Multiple Registrations.</u> Consider the advantge of offering discounts for accompanying spouses, for more than one person from the same or-organization, or for any relationship you can think

42

of that will enable you to enroll another participant that your program would not otherwise attract.
Don't be a policeman and ask for proof of the relationship, like a marriage license. A few people will
kindle a momentary relationship to get a discount but most will be honest.

Public Relations and the Help of Others

There are many ways to work with others to keep your
promotional costs low and extend the reach of your
advertising efforts. Many newspapers and radio stations
have a "Calendar of Events" or "Weekly Schedule" section
that will list your program at no charge. For real-estate
seminars, for example, newspapers will often provide a free
listing in the real estate section as a public service.

Appearing on radio and television talk shows to discuss
your program as a news event is an excellent way to
increase your exposure, while stirring a wider general
interest in your topic. Hosts of these shows will usually
ask for all the pertinent details of your operation without
any prompting on your part. Local newspapers often run feature articles on businesses that offer unique services
likely to interest their readers. Making the effort to keep
informed about local resources and public relations opportunities also has the desirable effect of producing a
network of contacts within the business and media
communities. The advantages of this kind of "networking"
have been described in detail elsewhere, so suffice it to
say that the contacts made through this informal network
can often prove to be invaluable resources in unexpected
ways, and are well worth cultivating.

Sharing advertising and mailing costs with other concerns can often result in significant savings for all
parties, without diminsihing the impact of the message.
There are formal cooperative mailings, listed in Standard
Rate & Data's "Direct Mail Lists Rates & Data," that will
insert your promotion into a joint mailing at a nominal
cost, usually a small fraction of the cost of doing your
own mailing. If you know other companies or individuals who
offer products or services that appeal to the same market
you are trying to tap, try sharing the costs of a joint
mailing or inserting your brochure into their mailing, and
paying them a fee or commission on the returns.

If you are working with a sponsor or client that qualifies as a non-profit agency, consider having them send the brochure in one of their mailings at the lower postal rate accorded to non-profit agencies.

People saying good things about your program to others is one of the best ways to establish a reputation that will continue to bring you new participants. In order for your past participants to be effective salespeople, your program must deliver what it promises and be satisfactory in every respect. An excellent product will deliver satisfied customers every time. The quickest way to klll a program is to present a session that does not measure up to the standards proclaimed in its advertising and expected by the participants. You may be able to fool some of the people some of the time, but the results of a substandard program will catch up with you eventually. Positive word-of-mouth referrals add to your credibility and reputation far more than advertising, since they come from known and trusted sources (friends and business associates), and they can't be construed as self-serving.

Sponsorship

A sponsor is a university, trade or professional association, or other organization which offers a program under its own auspices and pays the presenter directly, in one of several ways. A sponsor can add credibility and status to a seminar or workshop if the sponsoring organization is recognized and prestigious. If you are not well known and your sponsor is -- at least to your likely participants -- sponsorship lends the mantle of their reputation to your program. If the organization is nationally known, retaining their sponsorship as you travel throughout the country with your program could mean a readier acceptance of your professionalism and credentials from those who have never heard of you before, but who have respect for your sponsoring institution. If your sponsor is known locally or state-wide, only advertise their spnsorship where it is advantageous to do so.

To obtain sponsorship, a program must have the following characteristics:
1. It must be intrinsically appealing or interesting to the sponsoring organization and valuable to its members or to the market it serves.
2. The credentials, capablilities, and reputation of the presenters must meet the standards of the organization.

3. It should attract the quality of participant that the sponsor sees as beneficial to the long-term goals and objectives of the organization.

If you want to make your program attractive to a potential sponsor, it helps to understand his point of view, which may differ from yours. If you are in the business of designing and presenting original programs, you are probably entrepreneurial in nature, i.e. profit-oriented and a risk-taker. Sponsoring organizations are not likely to be risk-takers, so you will have to shoulder all or most of the risk and responsibility for the success of the seminar or workshop. The organization is probably encumbered by a bureaucracy; this means that you will have to walk the fine line between doing things their way and running your program in ways that your experience has proven successful. If you achieve this delicate balance, you will not only insure the success of your program, but also make your program a desirable asset to your sponsor.

Make it easy for your sponsor to want to work with you. Ask former clients and sponsors to write letters of support and recommendation about the effectiveness and success (profitability) of your program and the cooperative efficiency you showed in working with them. Remember, your sponsor is not a risk-taker, so anything you can do to lower the seeming risk of sponsoring your program will make you a more attractive candidate in their eyes.

There are more than 3,000 colleges and universities in this country, of which 1,600 have meaningful extension courses or continuing education programs. Most of these courses are taught by independent contractors who design and deliver an instructional program and are paid by the sponsoring college or university. The primary interest of most universities in running their adult education programs is to expand their academic and other offerings to best serve their students and communities. Although gross margin is not the main motive, it is certainly a consideration in their choice of programs, and the economic demands you make as a presenter must allow your sponsor to realize a reasonable return on investment.

Many, however, will accept a lower rate of financial return if their risks are low. This means that both your risk burden and profit potential are increased, which is as is should be, since whoever takes the risks of a program's success is entitled to a larger profit. This can be reflected in the payment options you offer to your sponsors.

You can simply charge them a flat fee (sponsor takes all the risk), or you can charge on a per-participant basis, either with a guaranteed minimum (shared risk) or without (you take all the risk). If your fee is tied to attendance, make sure you have control over the promotion; in this way you can exercise an influence over the factors that will determine your profit. If you are promoting through your sponsor's publications and public relations channels, offer your input to the design of marketing materials and press releases. Your help is usually welcomed, since your experience and marketing knowledge will help make the promotion more effective and increase participation, a mutual goal. It also means less work for the sponsor, which is another plus for him. Many promoters use a basic advertising format for the promotion of sponsored programs, with empty spaces to drop in the sponsor's name, date, registration, and payment procedures.

Whatever agreement is reached, the terms should be spelled out in a written contract. If your sponsor is a university, you will probably be paid between 30 and 90 days after the completion of the program. You may want to include a payment clause to expedite the payment of your fee, if you will be needing that money sooner.

Chapter 4
THE BEST YOU CAN BE

What to Call Your Program

Are you running a seminar, conference, workshop, or something else entirely? The nature of the interaction during a session determines what it should be called. The major training models are described below:

Audience Reaction Team: Generally consists of two to five trainees who react to a trainer's presentation. Members of the team are expected to interrupt the trainer to seek immediate clarification of unclear points, and to otherwise help the trainer to meet the specific needs of the trainees.

Brainstorming: A free-wheeling technique where creative thinking is more important that practical thinking. The format is to have trainees spontaneously present ideas on the topic (without regard to practicality), to jot the ideas on a chalkboard, and then to edit the list. An atmosphere must be created which will cause the trainees to be uninhibited.

Buzz Session: A method directly involving all members of a training group in the discussion process. The group is divided into threes for a limited time (about five minutes), for a discussion in which each trainee contributes his ideas.

Case Method: Consists of accounts of actual situations which are discussed with the objectives of discovering underlying principles, and applying the principles to diagnose and solve the problems. The purpose is to develop a problem-solving orientation among participants. Variations of the case method include the Harvard Method, the Incident Process Method and the Abbreviated Case.

Clinic: A meeting or extended series of meetings which involve analysis and treatment of specific conditions or problems.

47

Colloquy: A modified version of the panel (see page 50). The trainees express opinions, raise issues, and ask questions to be treated by the resource person.

Conference: A grouping of different presentations that offers several programs for the participant to choose from. Many authorities may present information in a variety of training models in each of the individual programs that make up a conference agenda.

Consultation: A deliberation between a trainer and an audience of one or more people. Included are telephone conversations, personal letters, and on-the-job visits.

Correspondence Course: A self-instructional course using print and/or non-print materials as the educational medium. Such course may include tutorial or small group sessions, consultation from a trainer, written assignments, passing examinations, and assigning grades.

Critical Incidents: Dramatized educational experiences in written, audio, and/or visual form which exemplify unusually dynamic, real-life events. They generally require trainees to make decisions and perform acts in a "laboratory" setting at critical moments in behavioral situations. The technique is used, for example, to teach foremen how to handle recalcitrant employees or to teach interviewers how to obtain critical information from prospective employees.

Demonstration (Method): A presentation which shows how to use a procedure or perform an act. It is often followed by the trainee carrying out the activity under the supervision of the trainer. It is basically a visual presentation accompanied by oral discussion, where psychomotor skills are taught.

Demonstration (Result): Shows by example the outcome of some practice that can be seen, heard, or felt. It often deals with operational costs, production procedures, or with the quality of a product. It generally requires a considerable period of time to complete.

Discussion Group: Includes a meeting of two or more people to informally discuss a topic of mutual concern. It is generally based on a common background achieved through assigned readings or shared educational experiences.

Exchange Study: Involves trainee learning through seeing a real-life situation from a vantage point different from that which the trainee would customarily experience.

Exhibits: Collections of related items displayed to assist in the learning process or to carry an educational, informational, or inspirational message.

Field Trip or Tour: Purposefully arranged events in which a training group visits a place of educational interest for direct observation and study. Field trips usually involve less than four hours while tours include visits to many points of interest and require from one day to several weeks to complete.

Forum: An assemblage of trainees used to facilitate discussion after a topic has been introduced by a speaker, panel, film or other technique. A moderator is used so that everyone has a chance to voice his views in an orderly manner.

Information Sheets: Commonly called "hand-outs." Learning aids given to trainees in support of a presentation. They may be in narrative or outline form, trainer-made or copied from published materials.

Interview: A presentation in which one or more resource persons respond to questioning by one or more trainees (interviewers). It is used to explore a topic in depth where a formal presentation is not desired by either trainees or resource persons.

Leaderless Discussion: A discussion session in which a trainer does not participate and no formal leader is designated. The method is most commonly used to overcome the formalities inherent in large classes through sub-grouping and spontaneous discussion in order to introduce issues or problems, generate involvement among participants, and provide opportunity for exchange of ideas.

Lecture (or Speech): A rather formal and carefully prepared oral presentation on a subject by a qualified expert.

Lecture Series: A sequence of speeches extended over a period of several days or as intermittently as one day a month for four months. The general format is for the lecturer to deliver a formal presentation while the trainees listen.

Letters, Circular: Usually not as personal as a newsletter, circular letters carry announcements, reports and training information. Such letters are usually printed or duplicated.

Listening Team: They listen, take notes, ask questions, and/or summarize a training session. The team is used to provide interaction between a speaker and the trainees. The team is especially useful where a speaker is not particularly knowledgeable about an organization's unique problems.

Newsletters: Are usually mailed to many people and carry messages which may be announcements, news or reports. They often carry training information and are the trainers' way of personally communicating with many people.

On-the-Job Training: Programs emphasizing learning by doing, normally under the guidance or direction of a more experienced person. On-the-job training is particularly useful in circumstances where new solutions to familiar problems are involved.

Panel: A discussion between four to eight experts on an assigned topic in front of a training group. A moderator insures that order is maintained, that each resource person gets equal time, and that the topic is covered in depth.

Programmed Instruction: A method of teaching, in a self-instruction format, using print and/or non-print materials as the training media. The trainer exerts his influence on the trainees indirectly through such devices as programmed textbooks, teaching machines, computer assisted instruction, dial access information retrieval systems, and other means.

Question Period: An organized follow-up session to a lecture or speech, in which trainees ask the lecturer questions. It is during this time that trainees ask for clarification of points made in the formal presentation and take the opportunity to ask for information which was not covered by the speaker, but which is of interest to them.

Seminar: Consists of a recognized expert leading a discussion among a group of trainees engaged in specialized study. The leader generally opens the seminar with a brief presentation, often covering provocative issues, and then guides a discussion in which all trainees participate.

Simulation: Contrived educational experiences, in various forms, which have the characteristics of a real-life situation. Simulations allow the trainee to make decisions or take action in a laboratory setting prior to really interacting with people and things. Examples are driver training simulators, educational games such as Monopoly, Blacks and Whites and CLUG (Community Land Use Games), all of which require actions and decisions by the trainees.

Skit: A brief, rehearsed, dramatic presentation involving two or more trainees. Working from a prepared script, the trainees act out an event or incident which dramatizes a situation taken from on-the-job experience.

Symposium: A series of prepared lectures given by two to five resource people. Each speaker presents one aspect of the topic. The presentations are brief, to the point, and generally do not exceed 25 minutes.

Workshop: A training method which permits extensive study of a specific topic. It usually gathers 15 to 30 people who meet together to improve their proficiency and collectively develop new operating procedures while solving problems.

Characteristics of a Good Program

An effective program will meet the following criteria:

1. It will provide information that is generally useful. People resent paying for a session that squanders their valuable time by presenting information which is superficial, unnecessary, or can be easily obtained elsewhere. The resulting unfavorable word-of-mouth publicity will make it difficult for this program to survive.

2. It will provide specific, "how-to" information, rather than theoretical concepts. Training should be designed to effect measurable change that will improve a participant's productivity, ability or practical skills, with a minimum expenditure of resources. It is not intended to replace or compete with a broad education generally provided by the regular curricula of colleges and universities in our society.

3. It will enable participants to get all necessary information in the shortest possible time. Seminars and workshops appeal to those who want a thorough understanding of a subject in a short period of intensive learning.

4. It will provide support materials to supplement the program. Materials should be designed to help a participant organize new information during the presentation, as well as access and review it easily afterward.

5. It will provide an avenue for further learning. A good program will pave the way for future study, either through a participant's own research, using the starting points provided by you, or through the resources provided in your materials — including any further information and bibliographic citations that you can provide.

6. It will entertain as well as inform. Humor, judiciously used in the context of the topic being discussed, contributes to a lively and interesting presentation, and it will enhance the learning process.

7. It will provide a "status report" to participants on a regular basis. Periodic summaries of topics covered will help people organize their new knowledge. Giving

51

quick previews of upcoming subjects and using question-
and-answer sessions will actively engage the participants in the learning process, instead of allowing them
to slip into a "passive recipient" mode.

8. It will provide an opportunity for the practice of
    learned skills. If a program is designed to teach par-
    ticipants new abilities, opportunities should be built
    into the agenda for them to practically apply those
    skills.

9. It will provide for participant comfort. Regularly sche-
    duled breaks will go a long way to alleviate restless-
    ness or boredom in your audience. Changes in training
    technique -- moving from lecture to exercise to audio-
    visual presentation to discussion sessions, etc. --
    will serve to keep participants interested and assist
    them in learning, due to the fact that different people
    are more receptive to different modes of learning.

The Length of the Program

The most important consideration in determining how
long a seminar or workshop should be is the time required
to cover the subject in sufficient detail. Some subjects
require two or three days to tackle the complexities of a
topic, while that amount of time would be superfluous in
others.

The burdens placed on the presenter(s) should also be
considered. In a single-day program, chances are that one
individual can handle the entire presentation. If it is
longer, either more presenters will be necessary or more
participant activity must be scheduled to ease the strain
on the presenter.

The cost to the participant is also a prime consideration. A multiple-day public program will be much more
expensive to the participant than a one-day seminar. The
costs of hotel, meals and transportation, added to the
seminar fee itself, can mount rapidly. The added costs and
difficulties of clearing busy calendars for two or three
days at a time can lead potential participants to look
askance at what is rapidly appearing to be a very large
expenditure of time and money. Programs designed for professionals and business executives should be compact. Far
more important than the fee for such participants is the
lost time or lost billings which result from their participation. A busy consultant, attorney or medical doctor
may lose hundreds or thousands of dollars a day.

There is a hospitality requirement on the part of the presenter that grows as the program gets longer. Providing suitable beverages and snacks and making sure that there are ample hotel, restaurant, entertainment and transportation facilities nearby greatly complicates the management of a program (as well as increases the costs) when it extends beyond a single day or two.

On the other hand, if your client is a corporation or other organization that is willing to give people time off from their jobs and pay their expenses, then a two- or three-day seminar might be more practical and lucrative. A longer program also gives people more time to absorb all the new information they are being presented with, and thus helps prevent participant burnout.

Another factor in determining the length of your program is the cost of renting your "classroom." Most programs are held in hotel or motel conference and meeting rooms. Hotels try to rent these rooms several times a day to maximize their profits. If your meeting will last an entire day, the hotel will charge you for those three or four lost opportunities to rent that room. This cost can often be absorbed by the higher fees people are willing to pay for a full day program than for one that is only a few hours long. Taking into consideration the hotel's profit motive and the public's perception of value based on the length of a program can result in a lower rental charge and higher profits for you. If, for example, you start your meeting at 10 AM and end at 5 PM, the hotel has the opportunity to rent your room for an early breakfast and an evening function. The rental charge will be less than if you had reserved the room from 8 AM to 6 PM, but the schedule will still be perceived by your particiapnts as a full day program, and the seminar fee can be set accordingly.

The Training Cycle

The training cycle begins with the recognition of the need for more information, and ends when the information is absorbed and integrated into an individual's working knowledge.

The amount of resources necessary to effect that change is the training requirement. The stages of the training cycle are as follows:

1. Recognition of the need for training or assistance. Public demand for a particular topic is often identified

53

by the seminar developer, although recognition of the need for further training may also come from an organizational client, either on his own behalf or from the personnel who will ultimately attend.

2. Determination of the need. The specific need is derived by pinpointing the exact nature of the concepts that must be conveyed to best fulfill the general need identified in the first stage.

3. Development of learning objectives. Learning objectives specify the new knowledge, skill or experience that the registrant will acquire as a direct result of participating in the program.

4. Establishment of information requirements. A subject is thoroughly researched to assemble the course content that will meet the learning objectives most effectively

5. Establishment of material requirements. Incorporate practical exercises into the agenda that will allow the participant to practice a tangible skill during the session.

6. Establishment of an agenda. Determine how long each part of the program will take. Plan for question-and-answer sessions.

7. Development of participant and trainer materials. Your participant materials should meet two criteria: aid to the learning process, and assistance in selling the program to others who will see them. The written materials should provide tangible "nuts and bolts" information that will reinforce the verbal presentation. It is also a good idea to leave room for note-taking, either in the margins or throughout the outline of the text. Since people are less inclined to lend or give away materials that include personal notes, this can have the desirable effect of piquing the interest of their friends and colleagues, who must then come to you for further information.

8. Design of an evaluation system. After the presentation, ask participants to evaluate the program elements and presenter skills. Give them the option of commenting anonymously, and ask for specific information that will be useful to you in making changes for future presentations.

9. Conduct of the program. Present the information in the program modules to the group, according to your agenda.

10. Report of results. A summary report is useful to trace and direct the evolution of a seminar or workshop, by

keeping track of ideas tested, rejected or accepted. In a captive program, a summary report may be part of the contractual obligations of the presenter.

11. Follow-up. After a suitable period of time has elapsed, a presenter may wish to do a follow-up evaluation, for two reasons:
    a) To test the long-term efficacy of the training, and consider program changes based on the results.
    b) To see if the demand for information has continued to grow to a level that may require further services in the form of additional programs or materials, which can then be marketed to the individual participant or client organization.

Seminar Materials

The possible places from which to obtain seminar materials are limited only by your creativity and imagination. Here are some suggestions to start you off:

1. Develop your own. This is often the best option, since the material will be specific to your needs and congruent with your course outline.
2. Book extracts, magazines, and professional journals can be excellent sources of supplemental material; publishers are usually generous with their permissions and low-cost reprints when the articles are used for educational purposes. Permission is usually necessary, and full credit should be given to the original source.
3. Materials from the Government Printing Office, which churns out vast quantities of information that is either free or low cost. Materials published by the government are in the public domain and can be reproduced without seeking permission.
4. Expert assistance from the government. That's right. Your tax dollars have bought you accecss to a panoply of government experts on just about any topic you can think of.
5. Trade and professional associations, banks, and insurance companies typically produce a wealth of undiscovered written information that may be just what you are looking for.
6. Simply investigating available resources through the reference section of a local library will usually turn up a myriad of possible sources.
7. There are many companies that are in the business of producing training materials, often free or at low cost

if they are developed under the auspices of an educational program.

8. Audiovisual aids. The use of audiovisual aids will enhance your prgram by providing a change of pace and an alternate way of learning that is effective and enjoyable to a society weaned on television and film. There is a dazzling array of sophisticated a/v equipment, materials and techniques to choose from. Any plan to invest a substantial amount of developmental dollars into a/v materials should be undertaken slowly and begun by a thorough investigation into the many options, their capablities, and long-run costs. During the testing stage of a program, it is not necessary to invest a great deal in fancy a/v materials or elaborate participant materials. Your participants don't know what your materials will look like when they sign up for the session, and it is not a critical factor in their satisfaction or dissatisfaction with the seminar. As long as the material presents needed information in a well-organized format, it will serve its function well. Simple and inexpensive audiovisual aids will also make it easier and less expensive to adapt your agenda quickly to changing conditions -- a flexibility that is crucial during the testing stage.

Advance Planning

A little advance planning can go a long way toward making your program run smoothly, and will avert last-minute problems. Try to have all your material ready to ship several weeks before the program date, so you can ship it ahead inexpensively by book postal rate and confirm its arrival at the hotel before you leave your home city. If your programs are scheduled close together or you don't have the time to do this, your only option is to take the materials on the plane with you. Airlines may or may not charge you for the extra baggage, depending on how sorely they need the traveler's business that week. If their profits are down, they charge for anything over the maximum weight limit, but you can often avoid this charge by enlisting the aid of a skycap. He may send your luggage right through at a cost of only a $10 or $20 tip, instead of the $30 to $50 excess-luggage charge you would have otherwise.

Hire reliable temporary help to run the registration desk at your seminar or workshop. This is much less expensive than bringing someone with you and paying their salary and travel expenses. If you request help in advance from two different temporary employment agencies and confirm the day before the program, you can be reasonably sure that at least one person will show up, so you won't wind up handling registrations yourself. Reserve that pre-seminar time for trouble-shooting any problems that may arise, meeting your participants and reviewing your materials.

Request from the employment agencies someone with top marketing skills, and indicate that you are willing to pay a little extra to guarantee that competent and qualified people show up on the day of your program. It is important to have good temporary help, because this initial contact sets a reassuring professional tone that creates a receptive environment for your presentation, and it gets you off to a good start.

Continuing Education Units

Many programs can qualify for continuing education units. These are criteria that have been established by various professional and trade groups, licensing boards and bureaus for continuing education credits for their members or licensees. These credits can often be applied to mandatory or optional requirements for continuing education in a given field. They are well worth investigating, since accreditation can increase your recognition, credibility and attendance. The time to determine whether a program can qualify for this kind of accreditation is before much developmental effort has been expended so that your curriculum can be geared to meet the requirements from the start.

Travelling Light

At each stage in the planning of the promotion and conduct of your seminar or workshop, consider what its execution will add to your administrative load. There are very real advantages to travelling light in this business, and simplicity should be a key factor in all your planning. Before setting up an elaborate bookkeeping system, for instance, ask yourself how much of that information is really necessary, and then pare away all the non-essentials. Be selfish with your administrative time. Don't construct an edifice whose maintenance will tie you to a desk for more hours a week than are strictly necessary. Hiring only indispensable personnel and producing only useful and profitable materials will also keep your travel expenses and overhead down. But the most important reason is that only by constantly honing the essentials and sweeping away the detritus will your seminar keep the sharp competitive edge that is necessary for survival.

The "Don't Forget" Checklist

Our survey respondents were asked to identify the three things most frequently overlooked in the planning and conduct of seminars and workshops. The following checklist reflects the common items named by at least 60% of the respondents:

* Schedule and conduct a meeting in advance of the program for the presenters.
* Have extra copies of presentation outlines and visuals in the event of loss.
* Test out presenters before turning them loose on your participants.
* Have back-up presenters available in the event planned presenters cannot make it.
* Repeat all participant questions and answers from the podium for the benefit of the group.
* Ensure that presenters don't duplicate, but complement one another.
* Train your presenters and orient them to your participant group.
* Keep on schedule. Don't allow breaks to drag on past scheduled time.
* In workshops and interactive programs, provide as much physical space as is reasonable between large group and small group activities. Give your participants a travel break, but don't mnake the trip too long.
* Maintain eye contact with participants — don't read.
* Potential participants will phone for information — be sure that phone personnel are informed about all program particulars.
* Acknowledge mail and phone registrations.
* Have name tags or cards typed on a convention typewriter or an IBM Selectric using the "Orator" typeface.
* Obtain temporary help for on-site clerical and registration purposes from at least two different agencies to ensure that at least one person will show up.
* After confirming in advance that your materials have arrived, find out exactly where in the hotel they will be.

Chapter 5
THE PLAYERS

The Participant

To attract people into your program, you must first understand their motivation for attending. Why would they want to come? Any of the following reasons, or combination of them, could spur an individual or organizational decision to attend your program:

1. The desire to learn. This could be triggered by personal interests or professional ambitions.
2. The desire to make more money. Learning new ways to increase wealth or save/maintain past accumulations of wealth is a powerful motivation for many.
3. Self-recognition of limitations.
4. Feelings of failure. A sensible approach to combat feelings of failure is to acquire a solid foundation in the perceived area of weakness.
5. Change of organizational or personal priorities. This can lead to a need or desire to expand one's horizons.
6. Change in job description or working conditions. The dynamic nature of the workplace often requires individuals to expand their career roles or change professions entirely.
7. New or added personnel. This can create a need for training, which may be as casual as on-the-job training or as formal as a degree program at a college of university (captive program).
8. Ineffective or inefficient procedures. These can lead to a need for training, although they can also be handled by better management, increased proceduralization or reduction of the human element. Training is often the preferred solution, since it reaches the root of the problem and develops human resources within an organization.
9. Mandates of government or trade and professional associ-

ations. These can change the body of knowledge needed to complete a given task.

Good Participant/Presenter Relations

The first opportunity you have in which to establish a positive image with your potential participants is with your brochure or ad. Does it convey the right impression and answer all the reader's likely questions? The favorable impression that your brochure leaves them with should be affirmed by their next contact with you: their reservation. If they are calling a toll-free number you have provided, they should be able to get through with ease and have their reservation taken quickly and competently by someone who can either answer any questions they might have or direct them elsewhere for the desired information. If someone responds -- either through business-reply mail or by telephone -- a letter of confirmation will reassure him that his reservation has been received; this will add weight to your image of professionalism and thoroughness. Include with the confirmation notice of all the pertinent details and another brochure, in case they lost the first one, returned it with their reservation or gave it to a friend.

When your participants arrive at the hotel make it easy for them to find you. The program should be posted prominently on the hotel's lobby meeting board. It's a good idea to check the wording scrupulously, since it will often be incorrectly posted; indeed it is often not listed at all. If you can't get someone in the hotel to change it, set up your own sign in the lobby, with the name, room number, date and time filled into the spot that you left conveniently blank for just that purpose. Once your registrants find the meeting room, have coffee (or whatever hospitality is appropriate for that time of day) waiting for them. This gives them something to do for a few minutes while they get used to their new surroundings.

The registration process should be handled as expeditiously as possible. Participants will already know their paynment options because you've specified them in the brochure. You will have hired one or two competent people from local temporary help agencies for the day, and you will have thoroughly briefed them on procedures before registration begins. If possible, be in the registration area to meet your participants, answer questions and make sure the registration process is going smoothly.

On occasion, you may be faced with someone who is dissatisfied with you program. Have a policy prepared in advance to deal with the unhappy participant. Most misunderstandings can be avoided by being very specific in the program description in your advertising, so that people have a clear idea of what to expect if they attend. Make your policy known in the materials, letter of confirmation or at the beginning of the program, as appropriate - - and stick to it. My own policy is to offer a money-back guarantee for any participant who is not satisfied with the program by the first coffee-break, or ninety minutes into the program. Very few people will avail themselves of this opportunity, but the policy is reassuring to the participant who is not a risk-taker. It also leaves you free to concentrate on your presentation, rather than be diverted by the necessity of making quick, last-minute decisions. And it eliminates the risk of misunderstandings with an unhappy client resulting from your policy not being clearly understood at the outset.

A firm policy on the use of tape recorders during your session should also be included in your promotion or confirmation. Many presenters have a firm rule against allowing others to record at their sessions, partly because the clicking and fumbling can be distracting to other participants and annoying to the presenter. Also, if a presenter is selling tapes of the session or providing them as part of the materials for the program, he would probably choose not to permit the use of individual recorders.

Yet, allowing a live recording of your program to participants can be an excellent resource for continued learning after the completion of the program. It may cost you some participants because people will share them with their friends, but it will also help spread word-of-mouth referrals for your program and win you new participants with no advertising expense on your part. Whether you elect to provide tapes or whether you allow individual recording, maintain your position consistently and inform your participants of your policy before they arrive at the meeting.

To help keep your fee lower, you may wish to sell a live recording of your program to participants. This allows those who feel they would benefit to obtain the tapes without burdening other participants with the additional costs. It is not necessary to record each presentation of your program. Recording one presentation and making the tapes available for sale at subsequent programs is sufficient. If you desire live recording of a program with on-the-spot duplication and delivery of tapes to participants, there are firms in every city that specialize in this type of service. Generally speaking, recording should not be looked upon as a casual activity. Professional personnel should be retained, and their references should be carefully checked.

In some of my own programs I have successfully used a dual pricing structure. A lower fee is charged for the seminar and outline, and a higher fee is charged for the complete package -- seminar, outline, cassette tapes, a handbook, follow-up consultation, meal, and other amenities. Some people like to fly first-class; others prefer coach. One advantage of the dual pricing structure is that participants are attracted to the program at the lower price, but during the emotion of onsite registration or later in the program they opt to upgrade to the complete package. This psychology has been used effectively in selling automobiles for years. It explains why low prices for cars are advertised, but dealer showrooms highlight deluxe models.

There may be times when you don't want to answer questions from the floor. Perhaps a question is out of context and will interrupt an idea you are trying to explain at that moment. Or the question may concern material that you plan to cover in greater depth later. There are a couple of ways to deal with this. You can simply defer the question by saying that you will answer it later. This allows you to maintain the flow of your presentation, but chances are that you will lose the attention of the questioner until you finally answer and satisfy his curiosity. In most cases, the best thing to do is simply answer the question. You can reply briefly, saying you'll get back to it in greater depth later on in the schedule, if you don't want to address the entire issue at that time. But, most important, by answering questions when they are asked, you acknowledge the right of the participants to an active role in the learning process; this is a critical factor for participant satisfaction with your seminar or workshop.

After you have presented your program a number of times, you will have been asked 95% of the questions you will ever be asked. You will find yourself anticipating questions before they are asked and answering them before they are raised. You must make every attempt to resist this tendency! Making your program too "pat" and inflexible removes its spontaneity and freshness and robs your participants of the opportunity for interaction. Another way of dealing with unwanted questions is to temporarily ignore them. With effective "visual directing" you can almost look through or past a raised hand, giving you time to make a point without seeming insensitive to participant needs.

Be alert for speech-makers. They can ruin your program. Some people are pleased to pay the registration fee to gain an opportunity to conduct their own seminars. These people don't ask questions, but instead make speeches. They are on their own ego trips. What they have to say is largely irrelevant and a waste of time. They bore your partricipants who came to listen to you. You must develop the skill of turning these people off without embarrassing them. One way to do this is to provide a short answer and, without stopping, continue with your agenda. Use their question or comment as a bridge to the next point you were planning to make anyway.

It is appropriate in some programs to present awards or certificates of achievement at the end of the program, or after the successful completion of an evaluation or test. It can make for good public relations, since these certificates often wind up framed and hung on a wall someplace where others can see them.

Program evaluations and follow-up communications will further establish your eagerness to elicit feedback from your participants, and your desire to improve your program. If it is a captive training program, use your evaluations to ascertain whether they came away from the program needing additional information that could have been incorporated into the program or could provide an additional service. Feedback is valuable in a public program as well, but you will often get that without a formal follow-up by such indicators as the onsite response to your presentation, word-of-mouth publicity and unsolicited comments.

The Presenter

If you can't unearth a subject in which your knowledgeable interest coincides with the willingness of others to pay for that information, take heart. Many successful entrepreneurs in the seminar and workshop business only understand the promotion and marketing aspects of the business; they wouldn't know where to begin to conduct a program themselves. You can have others present your program for you.

First determine if you really need a presenter. If you are just starting out, you may not really need one or be able to pay a fee or salary in addition to shouldering the extra overhead and travel expenses. Travelling with a contingent can get very expensive very quickly and you want to keep your road expenses low, especially during the testing phase of your program. If a full day or several days of presentation are fatiguing to you, try building some participant self-study materials, skill exercises and task activities into the curriculum to give yourself a chance to get some rest during the day.

Suppose you've tried all of the above and still need help, for any of the following reasons:

1. You want to break up into smaller groups and need someone to conduct them.

2. Your program is too long for you to do all the presenting without putting a severe strain on yourself, or it needs more diversity to keep your participants interested.

3. You have structured your program as a panel or forum that requires a presence of experts in various fields.

4. You want to increase the exposure of your program without increasing the wear and tear on yourself. You decide to hire someone to go to those cities you'd rather not travel to, or to speak on subjects in which you are not expert.

Now, you want to find the most qualified people at the lowest cost. The characteristics you'll need in an effective presenter will be different from those of a good developer. But before the presenter, you will need assistance with research; librarians and graduate students are excellent prospects for this activity and also for helping you develop an agenda and program materials. For assistance in presenting the program, you must first determine what level of presenter skills you will need. There is a trade-off between presenter skills and the sophistication of your material, as the figure on the following page illustrates. At one end of the spectrum, you will find some extremely well qualified people. They will be well versed in the subject, dynamic speakers, and able to very capably field any questions or situations that might arise. This kind of presenter does not need elaborate notes and materials, so invest developmental capital into the fee because he will also be expensive; save your money

The Presenter and the Materials

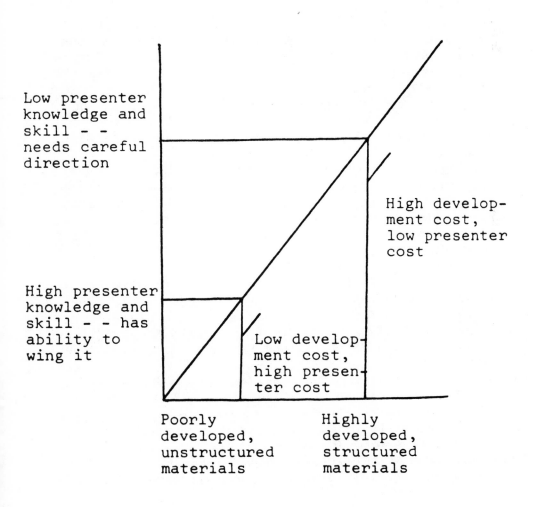

Low presenter knowledge and skill - - needs careful direction

High development cost, low presenter cost

High presenter knowledge and skill - - has ability to wing it

Low development cost, high presenter cost

Poorly developed, unstructured materials

Highly developed, structured materials

on the training materials. If your material is highly developed and structured, you don't need a walking encyclopedia
on the subject, because the program is carefully outlined
with all the necessary resources at the presenter's fingertips. If the program will be given only once, and any
material you develop has a short-lived use, it would be
wiser to put your resources into hiring the best presenter
you can find and letting him wing it. If your program will
be replicated many times with many different presenters,
then your best assurance of consistent quality is to
develop an elaborate set of notes that can adapt to many
indivual styles of presentation.

Once you have decided what kind of person you need,
where do you find people with the necessary qualifications?
Here are some sources, many of which are already at your
fingertips:

1. People you know. Most obvious and most overlooked. In
    your circle of friends and professional acquaintances,
    there is probably a wealth of talent. Make a list of
    people you know and their areas of expertise. Ask them
    for names of people they know in the field. This method
    is often used with great success in job hunting and it
    works equally well in reverse. You will be amazed at
    the range of talented people that you or your friends
    know.
2. Colleges and universities. People in educational envi-
    ronments usually have an excellent command of the lan-
    guage and the expertise and ability to get ideas across
    in a classroom situation. Higher educational institu-
    tions are hotbeds of talent and well worth your investi-
    gation.
3. Business and government. People in business or govern-
    ment who are prominent because of their position or who
    have written books or articles on your topic are all
    good candidates.
4. Advertising. By running an ad in appropriate publica-
    tions, you can generate many responses from highly qua-
    lified people.
5. Speakers bureaus. These are organizations whose func-
    tion it is to provide speakers with various back-
    grounds for seminars and lectures. This can be a fairly
    expensive avenue, but you have a high probability of
    getting seasoned professionals.
6. Your competition. You can tap the skills of other se-
    minar and workshop developers and promoters whose pro-

grams and styles of presentation you are already familiar with.

What kind of financial arrangement should you have with people who are interested in presenting your program for you? You can often find experts who are willing to speak simply for the exposure, and won't charge anything. There are many talented and dynamic speakers who would welcome the opportunity to speak to the group you have assembled for good public relations or to promote their own concepts or business, or to broaden their own experience base, or for any of a multitide of personal reasons. Explore the available talent you can tap at no charge or in exchange for a service from you.

If you are going to pay someone to present your program there are several types of arrangements to consider:

1. Hire them as employees. Before you do this, make sure you need their services all the time, not just when they are presenting programs. As an employer, your financial obligation to your employee is a steady one, not linked to your stream of income as it would be on a fee basis. One advantage of hiring people is that employees are less likely to be of an entrepreneurial bent than independent contractors, so there is probably less risk of spawning a competitor to your program courtesy of your training. Another way to protect yourself from this occurrence is to be sure that no single individual has complete knowledge and understanding of every phase of your business. Keep the marketing, financial aspects, field conduct and subject matter of your program separate areas of responsibility with your employees and colleagues.

2. Pay presenters a flat fee. In this instance, you take all of the risk, and if your turnout is large you keep most of the profits.

3. Guaranteed minimum plus a flat fee per participant. This is one of the most common types of fee arrangements, and shares the risk between the promoter and presenter. It gives the presenter a greater incentive to give the best program possible so that he can develop a long-term stream of income. As word-of-mouth spreads, more people attend the program, and he is continually asked back.

4. Performance contract. The presenter is paid on the basis of specific criteria, agreed to beforehand.
    Whatever the type of arrangement you negotiate with

your presenter(s), it should be in writing. If they are your employees, specifiy that they may not compete with you and describe what would constitute competition. If they are independent consultants, a contract should govern the complete nature of your association.

The agreement should have provisions for the following:

1. Compensation. The payment relationship should be clear and precise. Your obligation to your associates should not be contingent on the success of the program, your delayed payments from clients, unexpected program costs etc., unless it is clearly spelled out.
2. Character and extent of services. The responsibilities of both parties should be specified.
3. Period of service. It should have provisions for termination of the agreement.
4. Protection. The copyright of your materials should be protected by you. You should also set clear liability limits.

A copy of my standard agreement with independent consultants follows. It is an appropriate and advantageous contract for you to enter into with a presenter. In it you are referred to as "the Company" and the presenter is referred to as "the Consultant."

AGREEMENT

[company name] was formed to serve the continuing and specialized education of technical and other professional groups and individuals. Through its unique programs of presenting seminars and workshop offerings, [company name] provides quality education tailored to the specialized needs of professionals in a real-world, performance-oriented environment. The president of [company name] (hereinafter called "the President) desires to utilize the expert assistance of [presenter's name] (hereinafter called "the Consultant) in the field or fields in which the Consultant has special qualifications.

A. <u>Character and Extent of Services</u>

1. It is the mutual intent of the parties that the Consultant shall act strictly in a professional consulting capacity as an independent contractor for all purposes and in all situations and shall not be considered an employee of [company name] (hereinafter called "the Company").
2. The Consultant agrees to perform his activities in accordance with the highest and best state-of-the art of his profession.

3. The consultant is an independent contractor and shall provide workman's compensation insurance or self-insure his services. He shall also hold and keep blameless the Company, its officers, agents and employees from all damages, costs or expenses in law or equity that may at any time arise due to injury, death of persons, or damage to property, including Company property, arising by reason of, or in the course of performance of this agreement. Nor shall the Company be liable or responsible for any accident loss or damage, and the Consultant, at his own expense, cost and risk, shall defend any and all actions, suits or other legal proceedings that may be brought or instituted against the Company or officers or agents thereof on any claim or demand, and pay or satisfy any judgement that may be rendered against the Company or offerings or agents thereof in any such action, suit or legal proceeding.

B. Period of Service and Termination.

1. The period of service by the Consultant under this agreement shall be from [date] through [date] and may be renewed upon the mutual agreement of the parties hereto.

2. Either the Company or the Consultant may terminate this agreement by giving the other party 30 days written notice of the intention of such action.

3. The President reserves the right to halt or terminate the conduct of a seminar or workshop presented by the Consultant without prior notice or claim for additional compensation should, in the opinion of the President, such conduct not be in the best interests of the Company.

C. Compensation

1. Upon the Consultant's acceptance hereof, the Company agrees to pay the Consultant according to the following schedule: [Insert compensation rate or fixed fee and any allowance for or schedule of allowable expenses.]

2. In the event that the company desires, and it is mutually agreed to by the Consultant, the Consultant's services may be used in the conduct of seminar/workshops not specifically identified in par.C.1. In such cases, the Company agrees to pay the Consultant on the basis of the following schedule: [Insert compensation schedule.]

3. In the event of special circumstances, variations to the fee schedule of par. C.1. and C.2. will be allowed as mutually agreed to in writing by the parties hereto.

4. The Consultant will be notified by the President in writing to engage his participation in specific seminar(s) and/or workshop(s) to which the fee schedule of par. C.1.

and C.2. apply. Such notification will include a statement of the time(s) and place(s) of intended seminar-workshop conduct together with other information contributing to the successful conduct of the seminar-workshop sessions.

5. The Consultant, as an independent contractor, shall be responsible for any expenses incurred in the performance of this agreement, except as otherwise agreed to in writing prior to such expenses being incurred. The Company will reimburse the Consultant for reasonable travel expenses incurred with respect thereto. [A specification of "reasonable" may be inserted here.]

D. <u>Method of Payment</u>

1. Having proper notification the Consultant shall be paid as provided for in par. C.1. and C.2. hereof, on the basis of a properly executed "Claim for Consulting Service" form.

2. The "Claim for Consulting Service" form is to be submitted at the end of the calendar month during which consulting services are performed. Exceptions to this arrangement are allowed with the written approval of the President.

3. Payment to the Consultant will be made by check, delivered by certified mail postmarked no later than [specify] days subsequent to the receipt of the "Claim for Consulting Service" form as provided in par. D.1. and D.2.

E. <u>Copyrights</u>

1. The Consultant agrees that the Company shall determine the disposition of the title to and the rights under any copyright secured by the Consultant or his employees on copyrightable material first produced or composed and delivered to the Company under this agreement. The Consultant hereby grants to the Company a royalty-free, non-exclusive, irrevocable license to reproduce, translate, publish, use and dispose of, and to authorize others to do so, all copyrighted or copyrightable work not first used or composed by the Consultant in the performance of this agreement but which is incorporated into the material furnished under this agreement, provided that such license shall be only to the extent the Consultant now has or prior to the completion or final settlement of this agreement may acquire the right to grant such license without becoming liable to pay compensation to others solely because of such grant.

2. The Consultant agrees that he will not knowingly include any copyrighted material in any written or copyrightable material furnished or delivered under this

agreement without a license as provided in par. E.1. hereof or without the consent of the copyright owner, unless specific written approval of the Company to the inclusion of such copyrighted material is secured.

3. The Consultant agrees to report in writing to the Company promptly and in reasonable detail any notice or claim of copyright infringement received by the Consultant with respect to any material delivered under this agreement.

F. Drawings, Designs, Specifications

1. All drawings, sketches, designs, design datas, specifications, notebooks, technical and scientific data, and all photographs, negatives, reports, findings, recommendations, data and memoranda of every description relating thereto, as well as all copies of the foregoing, relating to the work performed under this agreement or any part thereof, shall be subject to the inspection of the Company at all reasonable times; and the Consultant and his employees shall afford the Company proper facilities for such inspection; and further shall be the property of the Company and may be used by the Company for any purpose whatsoever without any claim on the part of the Consultant and his employees for additional compensation, and subject to the right of the Consultant to retain a copy of said material shall be delivered to the Company or otherwise disposed of by the Consultant, either as the Company may from time to time direct during the progress of the work, or, in any event, as the Company shall direct upon the completion or termination of this agreement.

G. Assignment

1. The Company reserves the right to assign all or any part of its interest in and to this agreement. The Consultant may not assign or transfer this agreement or any interest therein or claim thereunder without the written approval of the Company.

IN WITNESS WHEREOF, the parties have executed this agreement.

CONSULTANT   COMPANY

Date   by
                                                    Date

[Publisher's note: The reader is advised to consult his attorney before signing any contractual agreement, since the author is not an attorney.]

71

Chapter 6
THE BOTTOM LINE

Those who are most successful in the seminar business test their concepts (program ideas and promotional strategies) carefully before investing large sums of capital. There are, as you know, a great many variables which can impact the financial success of a seminar or workshop. In my consulting practice, I regularly have clients contact me who wish to invest several thousand dollars testing a seminar concept. I always urge them to spend less. Virtually any seminar can be tested for $1,000 or less. They are amazed to learn that such low-cost testing is possible. When you are promoting through direct mail, the geographic location of your seminar is not an issue with respect to the cost of promotion. It costs you no more to mail across the country than across the street. Thus, if the cost of putting a promotional brochure into the hands of a prospective participant is say thirty cents, for $900 you can test market to 3,000. When, however, you are making use of mass advertising, such as newspapers, to fill your seminar seats, geographic location is a very important factor in terms of both getting good test results and keeping your market test budget under control. The following information should be helpful in this regard.

Selecting a Test Market
If a seminar succeeds in a good test market (town or medium-size city), it will probably roll out successfully on a national level in large cities. These are the important factors to consider when choosing a test market for your program:
1. Media availability: Non-compounding of media is the ideal situation for a test market city. This means that media in larger adjacent cities will not interfere with your test of the local media. For example, Santa Bar-

bara is an excellent test market for the Los Angeles area, although some people in Santa Barbara read "The Los Angeles Times." The local Santa Barbara paper reaches 60% to 62% of the market, so the "Times" coverage is not needed to reach a substantial Santa Barbara market.

2. Demographics: The population characteristics of a small city test market should be about the same as populations in your ultimate target areas.

3. Cost of the media: Again, if the local media is relatively isolated from the adjacent big-city media, you can save substantially on media costs.

4. Availability of facilities: Be sure the small cities you select have the facilities you require to give your presentation. You should be able to rent a suitable meeting room with the needed equipment, and the hotel must be convenient to transportation and restaurants.

5. Regionality: Your program may have greater appeal in some regions of the country than in others; this can result in some misleading test results. There are often inexplicable regional variations which are very real, and impossible to predict without testing the waters. Therefore, it is useful to test in a place where you're unsure about market conditions as well as on your own turf.

Choosing the Best Time and Day for Your Program

Our survey respondents selected the following months of the year and days of the week as the best times for presenting seminars and workshops (they are presented in priority order):

Business/Professional Programs (someone else is paying the bill)

March
October
April
September
November
January
February
June
May
July
August

Consumer/Personal Programs (fee paid by participant)

January
September
October
March
April
June
November
February
May
July
December

December	August
Wednesday	Thursday
Thursday	Saturday
Tuesday	Wednesday
Friday	Sunday
Saturday	Tuesday
Monday	Friday
Sunday	Monday

These are some of the factors to consider when selecting the time and date for your program:

1. Vacation periods. Attendance will suffer during heavy vacation periods, such as the month of August or the last week in December.
2. National holidays and religious holidays are also bad times to run a seminar or workshop. Also bad are major national or local events such as sports, political elections, etc.
3. Rush-hour traffic patterns, particularly in sprawling metropolitan complexes.
4. Use and availability of public transportation, particularly in large cities.
5. Air, bus, and rail transportation. If your participants will be travelling to your program by plane, bus or train, avoid peak travel days and times. Use some strategic thinking here. It is common for participants to fly in for a seminar in larger cities. The availability of relatively low-cost air travel and frequent commuter schedules makes it simple and worthwhile to fly in just for a single-day program. The high costs of hotels in many large cities, coupled with the additional cost of taking more time off from work than is strictly necessary, make it desirable for a participant to hop a plane from a nearby city on the morning of your program and return the same day. If such is the case, you would be well advised to schedule your program at an airport hotel and to start at 9:30 a.m. rather than 8 a.m. The slightly later starting time allows your participant to catch a 7 or 7:30 a.m. plane from a nearby city. He can then take a free shuttle bus to the airport hotel, rather than pay the (often considerable) cab fare from an airport to a downtown location. At the end of the day, the shuttle returns him free of charge to the airport in time to take a 6 p.m. flight back home. This not only avoids the tangle of rush-hour traffic that he would have to contend with in a downtown

location, but it also gets him back home in time for a late dinner.

6. Potential labor strife. Are the taxi drivers, transit workers, or hotel staff going to be on strike during your program? Ask in advance.

7. Will there be rooms available, or are the hotels booked up with tourist travel or conventions?

8. Events of major significance to your potential participants. Avoid conflicts with trade association or professional meetings for your participants or their clients/customers. The leading trade publication within a given field will list major events. On the other hand you may be able to take advantage of a national meeting in the same city by scheduling your seminar either immediately before or after, so attendees of the national meeting can also attend your session without incurring additional travel expenses.

9. Convenience of time and day. Some professions have, by tradition or workload, light and heavy schedules on different days of the week or months of the year. Take advantage of a perceived "light" day or month if one exists within the profession or trade your program is appealing to. Be sure to allow sufficient travel time for out-of-town participants.

City Circuits

Travelling in "city circuits" is a smart way to get the most from your media coverage and travel dollars. These circuits can best be planned for you by your travel agent. The savings to you in time (money) and travel expense can be enormous and will increase your profit considerably. These city circuits are also planned to take advantage of your media coverage, whereby a single newspaper advertisement may cover several seminars in several cities.

Weather is a factor in scheduling your circuits. Plan your seminars in different parts of the country around those times which will avoid severe weather conditions. Participants do not like or may be unable to sojourn in inclement weather.

There are some markets that can support more than one session of your program at a time, because of their large size, travel patterns or geographic complexity. Certain other markets can support a repetition of your seminar at several different times during the year. Dynamic, growing cities with big business and tourist appeal are likely places to repeat sessions as much as three to six times anually, depending on the subject. It may only be worthwhile to present your program once a year in smaller, less mobile communities.

Your seminar or workshop may also have profit potential outside the country. There are many foreign cities where fluency in English is widespread among the business and professional communities. Certainly any English-speaking countries are candidates, as are many cities in Western Europe, including Paris and most of the industrial centers of Germnay. Tokyo or Latin America might also work for you, depending upon the nature and appeal of your topic.

Selecting and Renting Facilities

The image you want your program to convey should be substantiated by the meeting site. First-class, quality hotels are important to most programs, and you should not skimp here.

Location is the first consideration in choosing a hotel. If some of your participants will be relying on public transportation to get to the meeting site, the hotel you choose should be in the downtown area and easily accessible. Safety is also a factor in choosing hotels in many urban areas. Crime in many inner-cities may be such a problem that a suburban or airport hotel is mandatory. This is particularly true if your program is likely to have a high percentage of women as participants. If participants will be coming to or leaving your meeting alone at night, a hotel located in a low-crime area that has restaurants and other evening activities nearby is a good choice.

How do you choose a hotel in an unfamiliar city? A good place to start is with a hotel guide. Immediately eliminate everything with under a three-star rating and all hotels in undesirable (for your purposes) locations. Watch out for hotel chains with multiple properties in a community. The many locations can be confusing to your participants, and they will end up scattered all over the city instead of conveniently gathered in your meeting room at the time the program is due to begin. For business groups it often pays to choose the best commercial hotel in town, because people in that communbity will feel comfortable about attending a program there and will have a receptive attitude and high expectations for the session. Take a look at what other seminar and workshop developers and promoters are doing. You should be on their mailing lists anyway. If they keep returning to a particular facility, chances are that they're getting the kind of service and participant satisfaction that you need for your program too.

Most major hotel chains have national sales offices, with branches in many cities. Booking through them will save you the expense of a few toll calls, but you can almost always get a better price by negotiating directly with the hotel itself. Most hotels have both sales and catering departments. The sales office handles meetings where sleeping rooms are involved; indeed, they base the meeting-room rate on the number of sleeping rooms booked. A sufficient number of sleeping rooms will get you the meeting room gratis. If you expect people from out of town, arrange for the sales office to block out a number of rooms at lower rates for your participants and for yourself. Hotels prefer to sell liquor, food and sleeping rooms. In order of priority, most hotels like to book functions as follows:

1. Conventions with sleeping rooms and catered meals.
2. Meetings with sleeping rooms.
3. Catered meals, which may include meetings.
4. Meetings without catered meals or sleeping rooms.

The priorities of the hotel business can present the one-day or partial-day seminar promoter with a problem. Some hotels will not commit space for seminars without meals and/or sleeping rooms until 30 days, six weeks or 90 days prior to your seminar date. They hope to snare a more profitable customer and don't want to tie up the space until they can do no better than the no-meal, no-sleeping-room function you want to hold.

If you need further advance commitments because you are a long-range planner or because you are promoting via direct mail, there is are two ways around such hotel policies. First, attempt to book at properties which don't handle convention business or large meetings. Second, some seminar providers tell the larger (convention booking) facilities that they will serve a meal or reserve sleeping rooms. Later, say 30 days prior to your meeting, they cancel the lunch and rooms. If you do this, remember that you won't be able to pull off this same act with a given hotel too often, but the high turnover with hotel sales and catering people gives those who use this strategy more opportunities than you might think to repeat this act, should it prove necessary.

If a program runs for a single day or a few hours, the catering department usually handles the arrangements. They get the meeting rooms that the sales department doesn't sell. So if the catering department says that they have no meeting rooms available, try double checking with the sales department before giving up on that hotel. If there are no meeting rooms, is it because of a convention that will lock you and your participants out of every hotel in that city, or just a busy day for that hotel? Let the sales office or catering department make your own room reservation for the night, because you will often get better sleeping accommodations for yourself with an in-house booking at the lowest corporate rate. I have often enjoyed the penthouse at standard, corporate, commercial rates as a result of such a booking.

The use of strategy can save you many dollars in renting hotel facilities. First, as noted earlier, deal directly with the local property and avoid the national sales office. Second, phone the catering (or sales) office to make your arrangements. Don't try to do it by letter — you can't be as strategic and it takes too much time. Third, ask for less than you need. If I need a room which will accommodate 50 people, I ask for a room which will handle 35. For 35 people, the hotel feels a bit uneasy (in most cases) about asking more than $125 for the day. For 50 people they feel comfortable about asking $200 or $250. The catering representative tells you that the Blue Room is available. Next, ask the rental rate for the Blue Room. When you are quoted $125, ask, in a surprised, shocked voice, "How many people does the Blue Room hold?" The answer will probably be 60, so you now have a room for 50 for $125. Had you started by asking for a room to hold 50, you would still be using the Blue Room but the cost might be $200. This won't always work, of course. Sometimes they will give you the Green Room which holds 35, and that only by force-fit with a shoe-horn. In such cases, you must tell the catering representative that you hate to be crowded, and you ask if they have a slightly larger room; it will now be the Blue Room, but the rental rate will probably be only $150 so you have still saved $50. Hotels generally do not have standard rates. They charge whatever the traffic will bear for their facilities. Being a strategic negotiator for meeting room facilities and guest rooms can result in appreciable savings on your rental costs.

Upon arriving at the hotel, double-check all arrangements and be prepared to manage your own function. It is a good idea to arrive the night before, since many hotels run their meetings poorly; include Murphy's Law as one of their managerial tenets. Expect to do it yourself, and view anything done in advance as a welcome surprise. Careful communication with the hotel about your program will reduce, but by no means eliminate, the mismanagement of your program. For all of my seminars, I mail to the hotel "set-up procedures," using a standard form such as the following. It helps.

MEETING FACILITIES: SET-UP FUNCTION
To: [name of hotel & representative]   [date]
This confirms our verbal reservation of [date]
[date of function]
1. Please post this meeting as follows:
    ——Consulting Seminar – Howard L. Shenson
    ——Seminar on Seminar & Workshops – Howard L. Shenson
    ——Information Entrepreneurship Seminar – Howard L. Shenson
    ——Grantsmanship Consulting Seminar – Howard L. Shenson
    ——Selling Consulting Services – Howard L. Shenson
    ——Advertising Seminar – Howard L. Shenson
    ——Newsletter Seminar – Howard L. Shenson
    —— ——
2. Please set room for [number] people.
    ( )Theater style( )Schoolroom Style [indicate which]
3. Please stack an additional [number] chairs in the rear of the room in case of need.
4. It is our understanding that we will be using [name of the meeting room].
5   Please provide a [size] head table for [number] persons at the front of the room.
    ALSO – – – PLEASE PROVIDE THE FOLLOWING EQUIPMENT:
    Table-top lectern
    Microphone [specifiy hand-held, lavalier or podium]
        If there is an additional charge for the lavalier mike, please provide hand-mike.
    Overhead projector for transparencies
        Place on head table. Do not order a projector table. Do not order pens or acetate. We acknowledge that there may be a rental charge for the projector and certain other supporting audio-visual equipment.
    Blackboard and chalk.
    Projection screen.

Additional materials required———————————————
——————————————————————————————————

6. Please set meeting room so that entrance is at the rear
   as some of the participants will be arriving after the
   start of the meeting.
7. Please provide [number] registration tables [size],
   [number]chairs, and [number] waste baskets. These items
   should be placed [specifiy locations].
8. The room must be ready for our set-up by [time of day].
9. If there is a telephone located in the meeting room,
   please inform your operator that no calls are to be put
   through between the hours of [specify]. In an emergency
   please have message delivered to the room.
10. Please provide ash-trays on one side of the room only.
11. Please provide water [specify locations].
12. The room will be vacant between the hours of [specify].
    Please use this time to refresh the room by providing
    fresh water, clean glasses and clean ash-trays.
13. FOOD AND BEVERAGE SERVICE
    Please provide the following beverages at the times in-
    dicated. [Specify types of beverages, quantity, loca-
    tion and times of day.] FOR BEVERAGE BREAKS AFTER THE
    FIRST BREAK, DO NOT REMOVE THE COFFEE. ADD TO THE RE-
    MAINDER FROM THE PRIOR BREAK UP TO THE MAXIMUM AMOUNT
    SPECIFIED ABOVE AND CHARGE ON THE BASIS OF AMOUNT ADDED
       Please provide the following food service [specify].
14. Please provide [number] standard, single guest rooms at
    your lowest corporate/convention rate GUARANTEED FOR
    LATE ARRIVAL AND MAIL TO THE ADDRESS ON THE REVERSE
    SIDE OF THIS FORM.
15. Please be advised that Howard L. Shenson has credit es-
    tablished with [specify chain or property]. Credit has
    been established with all major hotel chains, including
    Hyatt, Western, Marriot and Hilton. For bank reference
    please call or write.
16. We understand that the charges for the above services
    will be as follows:
       Facility Rental [amount]
       Beverage Service [amount]
       Guest Room(s) [amount]
       Other
Thank you for your attention to these details.
[Signature]
    Be sure that the room is suitable for your pre-
sentation. There should be easy entry to the room for the

convenience of all, and accessibility for the handicapped. Will it hold as many people as you are expecting? Many hotels have converted guest rooms to meeting rooms, or tacked on additional meeting rooms in barnlike structures accessible only through obscure passageways off the main facility. Don't make your participants take elevators, search down narrow corridors, or follow paper arrows taped to walls to find your meeting room. Converted guest rooms often have low ceilings, bathrooms jutting into the middle of the meeting room, and inadequate ventiliation. Old facilities are notorious for low ceilings, poor ventilation and support posts which can eliminate half of your seating if you have any audio-visual supports.

The seating arrangement will influence the cost of the room. A room set up theater style -- chairs only, no table -- as in most auditoriums, will hold up to twice as many people as a room set up school-room style, with a desk or table for each participant. The labor cost for setting up those tables is higher, too. Many people prefer theater-style seating, as long as they have a hard surface available to take notes. If the hotel does not have chairs with attached desk arms, you can package your seminar materials with a firm backing so that a desk surface isn't needed. For longer seminars (one full day or more) particularly where participants have work to do or notetaking, tables are considered more desirous. Check out the audiovisiual equipment you have ordered well in advance of the meeting to be sure that it is in working order. It is cheaper, but far more cumbersome, to carry your own equipment around with you.

Coffee costs can mount up surprisingly fast. A gallon of coffee holds about 20 cups, and you can save about 30% by buying by the gallon, not by the cup. Be sure the hotel provides small cups. I have rejected large 12-oz. cups in favor of 5-oz. cups on several occasions. People waste coffee. If they want a refill, fine, but don't encourage their wastefullness. Leave specific directions on coffee refills. If you are serving coffee as people arrive at 8:30 a.m. and the first coffee break is at 10 a.m., don't let the hotel take away the coffee remaining from the 8:30 break and sell it back to you an hour later. Tell them to replenish the original order. Pastry can be a big expense item, and most of it winds up uneaten. The majority of people will be just as happy not to have the temptation anyway.

81

Some prmoters run food functions, and include the price of the meal(s) in the registration fee. This can be advantageous because most hotels will waive or substantially reduce your meeting room rental fee if you are having meals catered there. There are, however, some significant disadvantages to getting into the catering business. It complicates the job of the promoter, makes a program appear much more expensive, and makes the promoter responsible for participant satisfaction in areas over which he has no control, such as the quality of food and service. If you provide an hour off for lunch, most people will wind up eating in the hotel anyway, but they don't think of the cost as part of the seminar fee, and they won't blame you if they are not satisfied with their meal. The cost to your participants will be less too. For a few dollars, the hotel coffee shop will serve them a nice lunch. When the lunch is catered, it can cost much more even for a simple salad or cold plate buffet.

Trying to save money by providing your own food or beverages is a mistake. Most hotels will not allow it, and if they do, they will charge you extra for it. They make their profit primarily from food and beverage sales, and they will go to great lengths to protect their interests.

When you are billed for the many services that the hotel didn't provide, don't just accept the hotel's word for it. Many hotels are notorious for their poor bookkeeping systems, so be sure to keep track of everything you ordered and actually received. Something as simple as a table on which to set your projector may cost you $20, and you may not have wanted it anyway.

Maximizing Profits in a Public Seminar or Workshop

To maximize profitability in a program open to the public, the price should be set at the highest level people are willing to pay to attend. Through testing or experience, a promoter tries to determine what, if any, price sensitivity exists for a particular program, and sets the price just under the amount that would result in a decision not to attend. The only problem with this theory, true though it may be, is the difficulty of translating it into a single monetary amount, since the valuation will differ with the individual and fluctuate wit' the unpredictability of the volume-price relationship. :f the price is raised, less people may attend, bu. the profitability per participant is higher. If the price is lowered, enrollment may increase, but direct costs will rise also due to the increased number of participants. The ideal you are seeking is the price at which the volume-price see-saw stabilizes at its most profitable level, and it may take some testing to determine what that point is and how to reach it.

A price schedule rather than a single price is useful to capture a share of the market that would not otherwise attend. Early registration discounts, special deals for spouses, co-workers, club members, etc., can all be effective in adding participants to a program. But if the price schedule is too complex, it will be self-defeating, since this secondary market will be even less inclined than your primary audience to wade through a lot of verbiage to figure out how much it will cost them to attend. The length of the program, time of day it is offered, and the quantity of program materials will all affect the price you charge. People are willing to pay more for a program that is perceived as complete and substantial.

Here is an example of a public seminar cost sheet to show you how to calculate the profit potential and break-even point:

Public Seminar/Workshop Cost Sheet

Expenses: Fixed	
Direct Mail prmotion (3,000 @ 35 cents)	$1,050
Trade publication advertising (2 @ $450)	900
Hotel conference room	200
Audiovisual rentals	70
Clerical support for onsite registration	110
Round trip air service	277
Ground Transportation	50
Seminar leader's hotel room	55
Seminar leader's meals, tips, & misc.	60
Total fixed expenses	$2,772

Expenses: Direct	
Participant materials	6
Coffee breaks	2

Break-even Point	
Program fee (assumed at $150 per participant)	150
Less direct expenses	8
Contribution margin	$ 142

Break-even equals $2,772/142, = 19.52
    (20 people needed to break even)

Potential for Profit
```
Direct mail response rate (.015x3,000)              45
Trade publication advertising (.009x32,000)         28
Total expected enrollment                           72
                                                    ——
Total profit (72x$142 - $2,772)              $7,452
```

Explanation

Fixed expenses: This includes all promotional and conduct expenses of the program, except for the direct costs.

Direct costs: Costs of materials provided for participant consumption. In the example, the direct cost is $8 per participant.

Break-even point: To calculate the amount a program must make in order not to lose money, deduct direct expenses from the participant fee to arrive at the contribution margin, in this case $142. Divide the fixed expenses by the contribution margin to arrive at the break-even point. In the example, twenty people are needed to cover all costs.

Potential for profit. Determining the profit potential requires an estimate of promotional effectiveness. How many responses can be expected from your direct mail promotion and other advertising efforts? If the direct mail response is a 1-1/2% return, 45 registrants should result from the mailing to 3,000 people in our example. If the trade publication ad brings in slightly under 1% of the journal's circulation, it will ad 28 registrants, for a total of 72. Multiply the total enrollment by the contribution margin to arrive at the profit potential, or $7,452.

After the seminar, be sure to measure the actual performance of your advertising against the expected response. You can code your responses in a variety of ways to get the necessary information. If you use a business reply mechanism, put a different code number on each ad or mailing piece. When registering the respondents for your program, keep track of the code numbers so that you can tell which ad drew the greatest number of responses. If registrants will be tearing off the ad and returning it to you, simply insert your code numbers on the coupon. Or, you might indicate, for instance, in your magazine ad that reservations should be sent to Suite 35G, in your newsletter ad to Suite 35H, and in your direct-mail brochure to Suite 35J. If they are responding by phone, use different phone numbers, department names or extensions to code their responses. If they are registering at the door, have a question on the registration card asking where they first heard of your seminar. Or you can instruct participants in your ad to tear out the ad and bring it to the seminar for a free gift. The gift need not be expensive. A few type-written pages on a subject of interest should be sufficient. Now you have their ad and need not rely on their memory for its source. The next time you give your seminar you will make more intelligent decisions about your advertising based on this information. An added benefit of having participants tear out the ad and carry it around with them is that it will help them remember to show up and register, and they will be more likely to show it to colleagues who might also decide to attend.

This point cannot be made too often: if a promotional avenue is not pulling for you, cut your losses and abandon it quickly. Concentrate on those prmotions where you get the most response for your advertising dollar, without relying exclusively on one promotion or type of media.

Registration

Typically, you should collect the following information on your registration form:

1. Name
2. Address (including zip code)
3. Area code and telephone number
4. Marketing information, i.e. "Where did you first hear of us?" or "What was the deciding factor in your attending?"

A sample of the registration card used for some of my seminars is provided on the next page. Note that the tear-off customer receipt serves as both a receipt for the transaction and an information source in case the participant wants to get back in touch with the presenter with any questions or for additional products or services. The objective of the registration card is to contain all necessary information in one place, and to provide a cross-reference to a simple cash-control system. The file number of the receipt is recorded on the check or credit card voucher used for payment, so that if a check or credit card is returned, it is a simple matter to trace the transaction back to its original source and decide upon the best course of action.

The information on the cards is valuable for building your own mailing list. Those who have bought your services once are prime candidates to purchase additional goods and

HOWARD L. SHENSON

SEMINAR REGISTRATION

FIRST NAME   MI   LAST NAME

ADDRESS

CITY   STATE   ZIP CODE

Area Code   Telephone

SIGNATURE   TODAY'S DATE

Do Not Write Below This Line

Card/Check No.   Auth./ABA No.

Pre Reg. Rcvd.   Mtls Ship   Will Attend

Paid   Bal. Due =   Rcvs. Mtls. =   Dep.

HLS

RECEIPT

Howard L. Shenson

20750 Ventura Boulevard
Woodland Hills, California 91364
Telephone: (818) 703-1415

AMOUNT PAID

DATE PAID

RCVD. BY

services from you. You can rent the list out, once you accumulate at least 5,000 names, to others who are eager to sell their goods and services to your clients, and who will pay between $50 and $70 per thousand for a one-time mailing to your customers. In certain instances, it may be more profitable not to rent out your list, but to maintain its exclusivity. If, for example, the company that wants your list will compete with your business, or if renting it out will hurt your chances for repeat business with your old customers in any way, you may be better off not doing so. This will also increase its desirability as a list with proven pulling power that has not been overworked, should you decide to rent it out at a later date.

Payment

You can arrange to be paid for the public seminar or workshop in any of the following ways:
1. Advance registration only. This will lower attendance, because it eliminates the participant option of deciding to attend at the last minute. It can, however, reduce the promoter's risk, since you know in advance whether or not the program will be profitable, and you can make an informed decision on the cancellation option.
2. At-the-door registration only. There are some advantages to this method. First, it suggests to participants that you know the program will be successful, and it makes your program more desirable. Second, you avoid having the expense and detail of handling pre-registrations. The disadvantages of not accepting pre-registrations are really only two. First, you have no idea how many will show up. Second, you lose the option of cancelling the program.
3. Advance registration and at-the-door registration. This is a good combination that reduces the promoter's risk without deterring late deciders from attending.
4. Checks. The risk of bad checks is low in the seminar and workshop business, and most promoters consider it an acceptable one to take. Accepting them will increase enrollment. Most checks that bounce are simply the result of sloppy bookkeeping, and their issuers will usually honor their debt.
5. Credit cards. Accepting credit cards is a low-risk way to boost your enrollment by 11% or more if the program appeals to the general public or business community.

Credit card companies issue "hot sheets" for stolen cards, which can be checked during the registration process. If a charge comes back to you because it exceeds the cardholder's established floor limit (the transaction amount above which telephone authorization of the charge is required), it can be re-submitted as multiple charges. Simply call the issuing company to determine their maximum per-charge limit, and re-submit the total amount on vouchers that are each below that limit. Write or stamp "signature on file" on the signature line of the vouchers (referring to the original voucher that the participant signed).

6. Extending credit. This will complicate administrative work, but credit can be offered selectively to reduce the risk of non-payment. Many seminar promoters will extend credit to recognized organizations, often by accepting their purchase orders, but not from individuals. Credit can be extended to individuals at low promoter risk when advance payment of the fee is required. For example, if someone registers for a February 4 seminar on January 5, and you acknowledge and bill him on January 8, then the fee is due prior to or during registration on February 4. Terms for credit should be kept simple; net 10 days, no offset.

7. Cash payments can be encouraged in the following ways:
   a) Have onsite, day-of-program registration. People don't send cash through the mail.
   b) Don't accept checks. This will hurt your enrollment and doesn't do much for public relations, but if the if the policy is spelled out in advance, those who wish to attend will bring cash or an alternate form of payment.
   c) Accept checks, but require credit cards or bank cards to guarantee them. Be certain that this policy is indicated in your promotional materials.
   d) Provide a separate line on the registration card for cash payments so that people are aware of it as an option.
   e) Provide a cash discount.
   f) Don't accept credit cards. This will hurt your enrollment, as was mentioned earlier.

Cancellation

You may wish to keep a cancellation option, unless you are relatively certain that the program will be successful.

It is difficult to know when to make the decision to cancel, because there's always the chance that late and walk-in re- gistrations will make the program profitable. Should you take the chance that enough people will show up on the day of the session to allow you to break even or make a profit? It may be worthwhile to hold a program even if it loses money. Since around 2/3 of the total costs are promotional ones, and since these dollars are long gone by the time a promoter is faced with this decision, anything that can be done to amortize that cost should be considered. Assume you've invested $2,000 in a program thus far, and would have to spend $800 more on program conduct costs. If you have ten advance registrants at a fee of $200 each, it is still worthwhile to hold that program, since an $800 loss is preferable to a loss of $2,000. The public relations impact of cancellation will be a negative one. So be sure that all factors are carefully weighed before deciding to cancel.

If your resources will not permit you to take a chance on running a program when turnout looks as though it will be poor, then set a cutoff date and set a minimmum number of registrants as criteria for cancellation, and stick to it. Cancel your program in enough time to meet the hotel's cancellation requirements, so that you don't wind up paying for facilities you aren't going to use. Cut your losses quickly if a session is not going to be successful; this will leave you with enough resources to take a different approach next time. The cutoff date should be announced in your brochure by saying something like "Your reservation must be received no later than December 31st."

Competition

The best way to avoid competition is to roll out rapidly. Once you have a workable program, move out quickly across the country and take a commanding lead in the marketplace before you are noticed by any potential competitors. As you go, continue to produce more product: more seminars, books, newsletters and information services. You will appear to be much too formidable to compete with as you criss-cross the country, entering every major market with a complete line of products and services.

One of the major pitfalls in this transition from a one-man band to an established institution is the tendency towards greed. Greed is the largest single cause of failure in the seminar and workshop business. Promoters spend too much on promotions to attract the largest number of people possible, and then they have to spend more on facilities and materials in case they all show up. A promoter must be able to say, "If this advertising pulls what I think it will, it will be enough for this session. I can always come back next month or next year and do it again here, if I don't overextend myself now." In the testing stages, keep the budget low, and don't worry too much about missed opportunities. They will be there waiting for you the next time around.

Maximizing Profits in a Captive Program

A proposal is the first step in winning a contract from a prospective client. The following items should be included in your contract proposal:
1. Statement of goals. Goals are open-ended statements of long-term direction or intent.
2. Statements of objectives. Specific statements, much more limited than goals, of the accomplishments that will be realized by the end of the training program. Future evaluations of effectiveness are based on the achievement of the objectives.
3. Statement of need. This may be a reiteration of the needs the client has already outlined, or the developer's perception of a client's organizational or personnel requirements. This is a way of coming to mental grips with a client and assuring him that you are addressing the same needs he perceives.
4. Statement of procedures. This includes the conduct plan, the time schedule, personnel capabilities and involvement, and promotion (if any).
5. Business proposal. This is often submitted as a separate proposal. It provides a cost-benefit analysis of the program, and it specifies fees and payment procedures.

Setting the Fee

There are several options for negotiating a fee that is satisfactory to you and your client:
1. Fixed fee. The client is presented with a fixed fee which includes the value of the labor of the seminar developers, the value of the labor of the seminar presenters and any additional personnel, overhead, an estimate of expenses, and profit.

90

2. Fixed fee plus expenses. The fixed fee excludes an estimate of direct expenses, which are billed in their
   exact amount to the client.
3. Per-participant charge. Since this method transfers the
   risk burden to the developer, it should be used only
   when you have control over the promotion of the workshop or seminar.
4. Per-participant charge with a guarantee. A flat fee per
   participant, with a guaranteed minimum of participants.
   This method shares the risk between promoter and client
   and is widely used.
5. Performance contract. Payment is made on a participant
   basis, determined by the number of participants who
   meet agreed-upon criteria after the training session,
   such as passing a test, skill sessions or evaluations.

Almost all corporations and government agencies have an
amount in mind that they are willing to pay, either
implicity or expressedly. That figure is between 100% and
150% of a participant's salary per day of training. Private
industry's figures tend to be higher than government's,
although not explicitly expressed. Government agencies will
often set precise figures which tend to be on the lower end
of the 100% - 150% range. A day's training can actually be
anywhere from 5 to ten hours. Very few single-day programs
are as much as 8 hours, but they are perceived as being
full-day programs anyway.

Perhaps the easiest way to understand the fee cal-
culation is to review the pricing sheet usually prepared by
the seminar developer. I always prepare one for my own purposes, as should you. However, it is to be used for your
own calculations only, and not revealed to the client.

Direct Labor
    Program Development
        Senior professional (10 days x $250) $2,500
        Staff associates (15 days x $150)   2,250
        Drafting (5 days x $80)   400
        Secretarial (12 days x $75)   900
            Program development sub-total $6,050
    Program Conduct
        Senior professional (4 days x $250) $1,000
        Staff associates (12 days x $150)   1,880
            Program conduct sub-total $2,800
    Total direct labor $8,850
    Overhead (at 90% of direct labor) $7,965

Direct Expenses

Survey instrumentation	$ 158
Telephone	200
Per diem (16 days x $150)	2,400
Air service (4 x $188)	752
Rental cars	225
Printing and photocopying	1,220
Other expenses	600
Direct Expenses Total	5,547
Sub-total	$19,562
Profit (20%)	3,192
Total fixed price	$23,474

Direct Labor — This includes program development and conduct labor. In the example above, the seminar developer estimates that a senior staff member will spend 10 days in materials and program development, at a salary of $250 per day, for a cost of $2500. Staff associates, at $150 per day, will spend 15 days on materials and program development, for a cost of $2250. A commercial artist or drafting person will work for five days at a cost of $80 per day, or $400. Finally, it is estimated that 12 days of secretarial time will be required, at $75 per day, or $900. The total direct labor estimate for this project comes to $6,050.

The program conduct costs will involve 4 days of senior professional time at a cost of $1,000. Staff associates will be needed for 12 days, at a cost of $1,800., bringing the program conduct sub-total to $2,800, and the total direct labor expense to $8,850.

Overhead — The cost of being in business, which includes such items as office expenses, taxes, licenses, marketing costs, stationery supplies, etc., is added in. The overhead does not need to be recalculated for every proposal, but the seminar developer should have historical knowledge of his overhead costs that can be expressed as a percentage of direct labor costs.

Direct Expenses — Next, the presenter must estimate the direct expenses that will be incurred. These are expenses that are generated by a specific client's project.

Sub-total — The sub-total in our example is $19,562. Assuming this program will train 40 people for 4 days, the total cost per participant day of training is $122.26. If this were a program offered by the training department of a corporation and did not need to make a profit, this would be the total cost of the program.

Profit — Add in your profit percentage (usually between 10%

and 25%), keeping in mind how much organizations are willing to pay for training.

The Contract Between You and Your Client

Once the proposal has been accepted by the client, perhaps after discussion and modification, the terms you've agreed to should be put into a written contract, which addresses the following issues:

1. Compensation: Specific amounts, time-table of payments, and precise definition of terms should be included. For example, if payment is based on the number of participants, is a participant defined as one who shows up, registers, or passes an evaluation test?
2. Responsibilities of client and presenter: Define in concrete terms the responsibilities of both parties, and any contingencies if they are not met.
3. Liability: Spell out liability limits for both parties.
4. Length of time: Specify the length of time that the agreement will be in effect, and provisions for terminating or changing the agreement.

Below is the standard, fixed-price agreement that I use:

[Publisher's note: The reader is advised to consult his attorney before signing any written agreements, since the author is not an attorney.]

AGREEMENT

THIS AGREEMENT is made this [date] by and between [client] hereinafter referred to as "the University" and [your company name], a [your state] corporation hereinafter referred to as "the Contractor."

WITNESSETH:

WHEREAS, the University desires to develop and conduct a training program for its personnel and the personnel of such other eligible education agencies as may become participants in this program; and

WHEREAS, the purposes of said training program are to: upgrade the managerial and technical skills of career counseling and placement personnel; and increase the professional stature of career counseling and placement personnel; and provide a cadre of trained professionals and appropriate materials to continue further training as required with minimum funding support needed; and provide a vehicle for the ongoing assessment of in-service training needs of career counseling and placement personnel.

WHEREAS, the Contractor is particularly skilled and com-

petent to conduct such a management training program; and
WHEREAS, funds for this contract are budgeted for and
included in a government project plan approved under_____
and as described in the program prospectus identified as
[name of grant], which is hereinafter referred to as "the
Project;" and
WHEREAS, said Project was approved on [date] and Project ex-
penditures were approved on [date].
NOW, THEREFORE, it is mutually agreed as follows:
1. The term of this Agreement shall be for the period
commencing [date], continuing to and until [date].
2. The Contractor agrees to develop and conduct a training
program consisting in part of a series of three workshop
presentations. Each of said workshop presentations shall be
of eight hours duration and shall be conducted at [place].
The aforesaid training program shall be developed and
conducted by the Contractor in accordance with the Project
prospectus submitted by the University for funding under
[name of grant] and in particular with the "attachment" to
said Program prospectus, which is marked "Exhibit A,"
attached hereto and by reference incorporated herein.
3. The aforesaid workshop presentation shall include three
days of intensive training using an approach which has
demonstrated considerable success working with career
counseling and placement personnel of this type. Specific
workshop topic coverage shall include the following: [list
topics]
4. The aforesaid training workshop will be conducted
during the contract term in accordance with a schedule
mutually agreed upon by the University and the Contractor.
5. In connection with the conducting and development of
the aforesaid training program, the Contractor arees as
follows:
   a) The Contractor will plan for and prepare such necessary materials as are needed to conduct the various program sessions as described. Such material preparation
and devlopment will include the preparation of participant resource material, worksheets, orientation materials, participant guides and handbooks. All materials
developed will reflect the highest standards of quality
applicable to educational material development.
   b) The Contractor will provide expert session facilita-
tion staff as follows: A minimum of one expert staff
for the first twelve (12) participants in attendance at
each session; further the Contractor will provide one

(1) additional expert staff for each addtional twelve (12) participants in attendance at each session to a maximum of 48 totyal participants per session.

c) The Contractor will regularly consult with designated personnel of the University for the purpose of monitoring program progress and planned activities so as to improve and strengthen the overall program.

6. The Contractor further agrees to:

a) Furnish the University on or before [date] with a final report. This report will describe all relevant aspects of program activity and will be in such style and format as to comply with the requirements of the enabling grant.

b) Prepare appropriate pre-session and post-session participant testing materials to enable the ongoing assessment of the overall program activities. The Contractor shall collect, analyze, and interpret these findngs as an integral part of the program development and conduct activity.

c) Conduct, within 4 to 6 months after the conclusion of the workshop presentations, a post-test follow-up survey which survey will seek to discover what difficulties, if any, the participants in the program have encountered in applying the principles developed in the workshop training activity to career counseling and placement problems. A component of the follow-up survey will probe for particular attitude and individual assessment of the relevancy of the workshop training activity and the topic material in the context of program administration experience during the intervening period.

d) Furnish the University with copies of all written and visual materials produced for distribution to the workshop participants. The Contractor will retain no proprietary rights to such material, said rights being vested to the University.

7. The University agrees as follows:

a) To designate one of its staff members as Project Director to represent the University in all technical matters pertaining to this program.

b) To arrange the necessary pre-program advertisement and participant notification so as to encourage participation.

c) To provide or otherwise arrange for facilities which are adequate to conduct the workshop sessions.

95

d) To limit session attendance, exclusive of Contractor staff, to the maximum eligible number of participants [insert number] plus up to three additional non-participating persons.

e) To make the necessary arrrangements with the participating educational agencies to make personnel available as participants in all specified training activities.

f) To arrange for the use on an as-available basis of University instructional equipment including 16mm sound projectors, overhead transparency projectors, 35mm slide projectors, tape recorders, and/or related audio-visual equipment as requested by the Contractor in response to program requirements. The University agrees to provide competent personnel to operate all such equipment. The University will provide adequate maintenance and care of such equipment and will provide operational assistance to the Contractor as requested.

g) To distribute to the program participants at the request of the Contractor, various project materials which are relevant to the program. Such materials may include training session handout materials, descriptive information, questionnaires and announcements.

h) To provide or arrange for assistance to the Contractor at training session locations as mutually agreed in connection with facility arrangements, scheduling, and other matters pertaining to the successful conduct of the program.

8. It is expressly understood and agreed by both parties hereto that the Contractor while engaging in carrying out and complying with any of the terms and conditions of this contract is an independent Contractor and is not an officer, agent, or employee of the University.

9. The Contractor shall provide workmen's compensation insurance or self-insure his services. He shall also hold and keep harmless the University and all officers, agents and employees thereof from all damages, costs or expenses in law or equity that may at any time arise or be set up because of injury to or death of persons or damage to property, including University property, arising by reason of, or in the course of, the performance of this contract; nor shall the University be liable or responsible for any accident, loss or damage, and the Contractor, at his own expense, cost and risk, shall defend any and all actions, suits or other legal proceedings that may be brought or instituted against the Uni-

versity or officers or agents thereof on any claim or
demand, and pay or satisfy any judgement that may be
rendered against the University or officers or agents
thereof in any such action, suit or legal proceeding.

10. In consideration of the satisfactory performance by the
Contractor, the University agrees to reimburse the Consultant in the amount of fifteen thousand dollars
($15,000) in accordance with the following schedule:

30 May 1987	$4,000.
30 June 1987	$5,000.
30 July 1987	$4,000.
30 August 1987	$2,000.
	$15,000.

IN WITNESS WHEREOF, each party has caused this Agreement to
be executed by its duly authorized representative on the
date first mentioned above.

CONTRACTOR   UNIVERSITY

name and title   name and title

Future Selling Opportunities

Selling additional products and services to your participants can increase your profits substantially, with
little extra effort on your part. You have already assembled your most likely prospects in one place. They are
an information-oriented group seeking to increase their
knowledge on a particular topic, who have already voted
with their pocketbooks to attend one of your programs. Most
of your selling job is done by the time this group is
gathered in your classroom. The average non-seminar profit
of the respondents to our survey who sold additional
products and services at or after the seminar was an
incredible 29%, — almost one-third of their total profits!
Anything sold in back-of-the room sales results in extra
profit that is equal to the value of the marketing efforts
that would normally have been required to make those sales.

What can you sell to your participants? First, look at
the information and materials that you are using in the
program itself. If your subject is a broad one, you may be
providing too much general, unfocused information. By
making your subject areas more specific and presenting the
information in more than one program or "information package" you not only break up the information into digestible
chunks, but you also maximize the potential to turn former

97

participants into future customers. For example, if you're trying to provide comprehensive coverage of a subject in a three-day, $350 program, you might be better off conducting three or four one-day programs at $200 each. It will be easier for many to get away for a single day instead of three, and they can come back later to take other sessions. Offer the seminar materials from your other programs for sale in the back of the room, attractively packaged and displayed.

Developing your own newsletter, training package, information and consulting service, or books is much more profitable than selling someone else's, although you may want to start out by selling other companies' products. The manufacturing costs of producing your own materials tend to be low, with the big expense in marketing, which you are eliminating in back-of-the-room sales. When you buy from major publishers, even at the 40% to 60% discount that most of them will offer, their selling costs are built into the price of their products. Since you are doing their selling for them, that translates into an extra margin of profit for them. By selling your own products, the money saved on marketing costs becomes extra profit for you.

There are many companies that consider your participants a primary market for their goods and services; they will rent space from you at your meeting site to sell their books, hardware or training programs. This is more often done with multi-day conferences than with one-day seminars, but it can be done in both situations to defray or completely pay for the rental costs of your classroom. The disadvantages of renting out space are that it requires you to rent more space initially, it creates another complicating factor in your administrative life, and it takes participant time and attention away from your program.

The best strategy to convince your participants of the worth of your information products is to present a good program. Concentrating on practical, useful information is the best guarantee that your other products and services will do the same. It's not necessary to do a "hard sell" to a professional, information-oriented group, and it may in fact turn them off. Your presentation and the products will largely speak for themselves. If you do mention the availability of additional materials during the program, wait until you have established your credibility with the group and a rapport has been developed. If you allude to them only when their content is relevant to the subject being discussed at that moment, it will pique the interest of your participants enough for them to take a closer look during the break. At that point, the material must stand or fall on its own merits. If the information is substantial and on-target with the needs of the group, it will sell.

Your sales will increase if you bring your inventory with you and complete the transaction on the spot. At the very least, you must have some handsomely packaged samples on display, since people are much more likely to buy products that they can touch and examine. A catalogue alone is not sufficient. Seeing these individuals absorbed in their purchases will also provoke curiosity and further investigation from your other participants.

Requests from your participants for your services as a professional after the seminar or workshop will be both common and lucrative. Selling your services as a professional to seminar attendees, if you desire to do so, is such a good opportunity that many people give seminars on a break-even or loss basis just to attract clients.

CONCLUSION

Developing and conducting seminars and workshops can be an enormously rewarding enterprise. Well done, it satisfies a desire to help others grow and learn how to become more effective in their daily lives. Its challenges are diverse; its opportunities for personal growth and gratification are many.

The financial rewards of creating and maintaining a consistently strong program are also considerable. A successful ongoing seminar has a net worth of between five and ten times its annual profit -- for most programs, between $200,000 and $600,000. By staying responsive to the currents of change, your program can only get better and more profitable -- a natural growth process fueled by assiduous testing and fine-tuning of the many elements of a program's promotion and conduct.

If this book has helped show you the way to turn an idea into a viable program, and a viable program into a successful one, then it will have served its purpose. If, along the way, you find that you have been challenged and you rise to meet that challenge, or if you've discovered the satisfactions of creating a new resource through your own ingenuity, then it will have done even more -- helped you to fulfill your own purpose.

ABOUT THE AUTHOR

Howard L. Shenson is an experienced, successful developer/-promoter of more than 200,000 participating training days for the past eighteen years. 25% of these were under contract to government, association and corporate clients; the other 75% were conducted in open-to-the-public seminars. This experience came from both his own proprietary efforts as well as work he has done for clients in his capacity as a consultant to seminar providers — large and small.

Prior to entering the consultant profession and seminar business, Mr. Shenson served as Chairman of The Department of Management at California State University, Northridge, and as Assistant to the Director of The University of Southern California Research Institute for Business & Economics. He also serves as consultant to numerous corporations, educational agencies and entrepreneurs on the dvelopment and promotion of seminars, workshops and related educational events.

He has authored several books, journal and magazine articles and audio-cassette training packages, and is editor/publisher of "The Professional Consultant & Seminar Business Report."

Mr. Shenson maintains his offices in Woodland Hills, California, located in the San Fernando Valley section of the city of Los Angeles, just a few miles from his home, where he resides with his wife and three sons.